THE ESSENTIAL MANUAL FOR ASPERGER SYNDROME (ASD) IN THE CLASSROOM

by the same author

Inside Asperger's Looking Out
ISBN 978 1 84905 334 1
eISBN 978 0 85700 670 7

All Cats Have Asperger Syndrome
ISBN 978 1 84310 481 0

All Dogs Have ADHD
ISBN 978 1 84310 651 7
eISBN 978 1 84642 840 1

Haze
ISBN 978 1 84310 072 0
eISBN 978 1 84642 405 2

Blue Bottle Mystery
An Asperger Adventure
ISBN 978 1 85302 978 3
eISBN 978 1 84642 169 3
Part of the Asperger Adventures series

Of Mice and Aliens
An Asperger Adventure
ISBN 978 1 84310 007 2
eISBN 978 0 85700 179 5
Part of the Asperger Adventures series

Lisa and the Lacemaker
An Asperger Adventure
ISBN 978 1 84310 071 3
eISBN 978 1 84642 354 3
Part of the Asperger Adventures series

THE ESSENTIAL MANUAL FOR

ASPERGER

SYNDROME

(ASD) IN THE

CLASSROOM

What Every Teacher Needs to Know

Kathy Hoopmann

Illustrated by Rebecca Houkamau

Foreword by Tony Attwood

Jessica Kingsley *Publishers*
London and Philadelphia

First published in 2015
by Jessica Kingsley Publishers
73 Collier Street
London N1 9BE, UK
and
400 Market Street, Suite 400
Philadelphia, PA 19106, USA

www.jkp.com

Library of Congress Cataloging in Publication Data
A CIP catalog record for this book is available from the Library of Congress

British Library Cataloguing in Publication Data
A CIP catalogue record for this book is available from the British Library

ISBN 978 1 84905 553 6
eISBN 978 0 85700 984 5

Printed and bound in Great Britain

For my mother,
who understands grammar and knows how to spell, and is
prepared to spend hours fixing all my mistakes.

ACKNOWLEDGEMENTS

With special thanks to Tony Attwood and Maja Toudal for giving invaluable feedback; to my father, who thinks everything I write is wonderful; and to my incredibly talented daughter, Rebecca Houkamau, for her quirky illustrations.

CONTENTS

Foreword

If every primary school teacher read this book, the lives of all young children who have Asperger Syndrome would be significantly improved. They would at last feel that the teacher understands them and thus feel so much happier, more relaxed and better able to achieve academic and social success.

This book really is an essential manual, covering all the issues associated with Asperger syndrome in the classroom. I would particularly like to thank Kathy for describing the social profile and strategies to reduce sensory sensitivity and for creating classroom activities that enable other children to appreciate what it is like to have Asperger Syndrome.

Tony Attwood
Minds & Hearts Clinic, Brisbane, Australia

ISSUE SORTER

In what area is your student facing issues?	Find this in...	
Social and Emotional		
• difficulties relating to others in social situations • difficulties making friends • difficulties understanding that people have different needs and thoughts • difficulties expressing emotions and understanding emotions in others • dislikes or has difficulties with group activites and sports	• Manners • Hygiene • Understanding the Perspectives of Others: Theory of Mind • Body Language Blindness • Forming Friendships and Following Social Rules • Apparent Lack of Emotions • Bullying	25 26 52 62 80 92 116
Verbal and Non-verbal Communication		
• a literal interpretation of language and has problems understanding sarcasm, humour and colloquialisms • speech and language difficulties • poor eye contact • poor self-esteem	• Manners • Understanding the Perspectives of Others: Theory of Mind • Body Language Blindness • Literal Thinkers and Speakers • Forming Friendships and Following Social Rules • Apparent Lack of Emotions • Bullying • Classroom Discipline: To Punish or Not to Punish	25 52 62 70 80 92 116 138
Behavioural Issues		
• ignores instructions • is disobedient and disrespectful • hurts other children	• Classroom Discipline: To Punish or Not to Punish • Sensory Issues	138 143

Preparing for Your Student with Asperger Syndrome

How to use this book

This book is designed to assist the classroom teacher in teaching and supporting a student with Asperger Syndrome. Although it is aimed at primary teachers, many of the suggestions will be valid for students of all ages. Each chapter is a guide to understanding common issues faced by the child and teacher and gives an insight into what the child is thinking and why she behaves the way she does. It provides suggestions for how various situations and issues can be dealt with within a classroom setting and gives activities to enlighten others about what the child with Asperger's is experiencing. Hints for parents and carers highlight ways in which the school and home can work together to provide the best possible outcome for the child.

Ultimately this book is designed so that the student can be understood and supported and the teacher can understand and support. It is not designed to be read from cover to cover but rather is structured so the teacher need only refer to the section relevant at a given time. For this reason, some of the suggestions and hints are repeated in different areas.

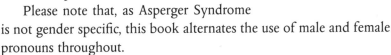

Please note that, as Asperger Syndrome is not gender specific, this book alternates the use of male and female pronouns throughout.

What this book is NOT

- It is not designed to cover every issue a teacher may face.

- It is not an individual educational programme.

- It is not written for specialist teachers to deal with complex issues arising from Asperger Syndrome.

It may be necessary for the teacher to seek specialist advice with specific issues that arise in the classroom.

What are Asperger Syndrome and Autism Spectrum Disorders (ASD)?

Asperger Syndrome is named after Hans Asperger (1906–1980), an Austrian paediatrician who identified a group of adults and children who had problems in the areas of social interaction and communication, and had sensory and adaptation issues.

Today, the criteria that doctors and psychologists and psychiatrists use when diagnosing a patient with Asperger Syndrome comes from the *Diagnostic and Statistical Manual of Mental Disorders*, commonly known as the *DSM*. This manual undergoes updating from time to time. The most recent update was in 2013 and is known as the *DSM-5*.

The previous version, the *DSM-IV*, separated autistic disorders into four areas:

- Autistic Disorder

- Asperger Syndrome

- Childhood Disintegrative Disorder

- Pervasive Development Disorder – Not Otherwise Specified (PDD–NOS).

In the *DSM-5*, all of these four disorders are now grouped under the term:

- Autism Spectrum Disorders (ASD)

and those people who have significant problems only in social communication are considered to have:

- Social (Pragmatic) Communication Disorder (SCD).

However, as the term Asperger Syndrome is still so widely used, for the sake of convenience, and for continuity with previous publications, the term Asperger Syndrome will be used throughout this book.

In general, a person with Asperger Syndrome is identified as someone who may have:

- difficulties relating to others in social situations
- difficulties understanding verbal and non-verbal communication
- a literal interpretation of language, and problems understanding sarcasm and colloquialisms
- speech and language difficulties
- heightened sensitivity to touch, sight, hearing, taste and smell
- difficulties with body awareness (proprioception) and balance (vestibular system)
- difficulties expressing emotions and understanding emotions in others
- set routines and a strong preference for order
- an intense ability to focus on specific interest areas
- difficulties with coordination and can be clumsy
- a predisposition for visual learning
- great loyalty towards others
- an inability to tell lies convincingly
- a unique mind which is able to see life from a new perspective.

But as you read, remember that not every person with Asperger Syndrome must have all the traits mentioned in this book, and they may

have some that are not mentioned. Two students with Asperger's can be extreme opposites in personality and behaviour and still both have Asperger's. By your understanding of their strengths and weaknesses and through your encouragement and support, your student with Asperger's can flourish and reach her full and wonderful potential.

Who is your student with Asperger Syndrome?

With up to one in eighty children now being diagnosed with Asperger Syndrome or ASD, there is a very high chance that eventually you will one day teach a child with Asperger's. Remember, the child does not have a disease and does not need 'fixing'. The most important thing you can do is push aside any preconceived ideas you have. Without any doubt, this child will be different from any other student or person you know with Asperger's, just as each student is different from any other. And teaching a child with Asperger Syndrome is just like teaching any child. The child has strengths and weaknesses. She wants to be valued and accepted and supported and will respond to kindness and anger in much the same way as anyone else does.

However, there are a few things that a child with Asperger's needs or benefits from, over and above your other students. One of the most important things to keep in mind is how hard a child with Asperger's has to concentrate at school. She has to: survive the complex web of social interaction and expectations; try to interpret verbal and non-verbal communications; deal with a multitude of sensory issues; and, on top of all that, still learn the day's lessons. Give the child a bit of slack. If she suddenly displays unusual behaviours, consider what may have changed in the classroom or environment or consider the child's relationship with her peers. Take the time to provide a few extra words of explanation about the task at hand. If you see the child fidgeting and irritable, allow her to get up and walk around or work standing or lying on the floor. Send the child on an errand to stretch her legs and to have a break from classroom pressures. Provide safe places in the classroom where the child can go for time out and make sure she has a place to go at lunch-times where she will not be alone, such as the library or in a club. If you take the time to prepare yourself and your classroom for your new addition, then both you and your student can look forward to a rewarding and successful year.

Are you the right teacher?

If you are open-minded, fair, consistent, flexible and are willing to seek the best in every student, then you can teach a child with Asperger Syndrome. Having a good sense of humour is also a plus. Some parents will ask for a specific teacher for their child. While it can be unrealistic for every parent to expect to get the teacher they want, the wishes of a parent of a child with Asperger Syndrome should be considered carefully as the child is less able to adapt and thrive under a teacher she dislikes or feels dislikes her.

Think positively

There are a lot of things you can look forward to in your new student. Children with Asperger's come with a bucket-load of positive attributes too. If you are fair, understanding and consistent, then you will have a model student on your hands who will name you the best teacher ever, for the rest of her life. If you stick to routines and are clear in your instructions then the child will be willing, obedient and helpful. If you permit your students to have a voice and to express opinions, the child will amaze you with unique perspectives and interesting facts. If you give the child a set job, you can be sure it is always done on time and done exactly the way you want it to be done. This child will be kind to younger kids and have a heart of gold when it comes to others in need, especially those being bullied. Her honesty can be refreshing and utterly to be relied on. If you tap into the child's abilities in games such as chess, and individual sports such as running and archery, you can have a school champion in your class. If your student is inclined towards computers then all your IT problems will vanish overnight.

And if you have a sense of humour, this child will make you laugh and bring joy to your day.

Preparing yourself and the classroom

- Talk to other staff who may have dealt with the child in the past. Be very careful not to form preconceived views of the child from the opinions of others. Use this time to seek out positive ways to help the child, and ignore negative overtones.

- Take the time to consider what your physical classroom is like for your student with Asperger's. It is very likely the child will have sensory issues. Is the room cluttered with things that will draw her attention away from you? Consider the irritation to your child from fluorescent lights, direct sunlight, a/c, fans, strong scents, hard floors, and so on.

- Do you have a place in the classroom to which the child can retreat if overloaded with input and expectations?

- Your student may not like being surrounded on all sides by other people. Can you place her at the end of a row, or the front or back, or even at a side table? When your student arrives, ask where she prefers to sit. Provide a space in class where the child can stand to work or lie on the floor.

- Stock up on items that may help your student relax and participate to the fullest. Have cushions that the child can sit on, both on the floor and at her seat. Provide earphones the child can use if noise levels get too high. Gather a box of fidget toys, such as squeeze balls, bubble wrap, paper clips, pieces of velvet or silk, that the child can fiddle with to relieve stress. Be prepared to allow the child to wear a hat in class or even listen to her own music when working on activities. Have a weighted vest or blanket ready in order to settle the child with body awareness or tactile issues.

Before the start of the school year

- Invite the student and her parents or carers to come to the school.

- Learn the child's name and check that you are saying it correctly. Sometimes a child with Asperger's will not recognize a nickname or a name said with an accent. For example, Robert may not respond to Rob or may only respond to ROBert and not RobERT.

- Show the child where she will sit and where to put belongings.

- If the child has a locker allocated, make sure it is at the end of the row so that she can get to it without being jostled from both sides.

- Explain where the child can go or to whom she can speak if she is feeling stressed or unsafe, for example the library, the nurse's room, the school counsellor.

- Provide the child with a map of the school and walk around the school grounds pointing out play areas, eating areas, toilets, positions of other classrooms the child may attend (music, science, art). Show areas that are out of bounds. Do this even if the child attended the school the year before, as orientating herself from a new home-room may be difficult.

- Introduce the child to other teachers and adults who may deal with the child, such as the sports teacher, music teacher, classroom assistant and reception staff.

- Swap contact details with the parents so you can contact each other whenever necessary.

- Encourage the child or parent to take photos on this visit so the child can look at the photos when at home to help remember places to go and people's faces.

- Explain that a class diary will go with the child to and from school each day. Show the parents where they can write notes to you and where to look for your notes to them.

- Provide a schedule for at least the first week so the child knows what to bring each day and what to expect when she arrives.

- Particularly explain what will happen on the first day. Let the child know how long her parents will be allowed to stay to help get her settled.

Hints for parents to prepare the child for the new school year

- Take the child to school before the beginning of term to meet the teacher.

- Get the child into the same bedtime routine that she will have during term at least a few days before school starts.

- Make sure the uniform or new school clothes are prewashed and are as comfortable as possible. Remove tags if necessary. Allow the child to wear-in new shoes slowly over the holidays.

- Arrange a play-date with another student from the class before term starts.

- Allow the child to be an active participant in buying books and pens equipment for class.

- Go over the first week's schedule as provided by the teacher.

- Remind the child of the morning daily routine. If necessary, make up picture charts of what the child must do to get ready (e.g. make bed, brush teeth).

- Look at the school map to remind the child where she has to go and where she can/can't go.

- Remind the child how to greet friends and adults.

- Go through photos of last year's activities, or look at the year book to remind the child of people's names.

- Discuss with the child the type of things people say to each other after a long break. Help her to know how to answer things like 'How were your holidays?', 'What did you do during the break?' Explain that it is nice to notice things about her friends, like a new hair-cut or new stationery, and this can help her make new friends. Remind the child not to talk about her special interest for longer than a few minutes at a time.

- Arrive on time to pick the child up after school on the first day – actually, most days – or make sure the child is aware that you will be late.

Parents have needs too

Never forget that you are teaching a child who is loved by someone.

Read that sentence again: Never forget that you are teaching a child who is loved by someone.

Parents love their children. Sometimes, as a teacher, that fact is easy to forget. If the child is difficult, disrespectful and disobedient then you will want the parents to know all about how hard your life is with *their* child in *your* classroom. Perhaps you even think, although you may never say it aloud, that you could do a much better job of bringing up that child than the parents are doing.

You would be wrong, of course.

When a child is diagnosed with Asperger Syndrome, it is well recognized that parents go through various stages of understanding and acceptance:

1. First comes some sort of grief as the parents come to terms with the fact that the child they thought they had does not exist. They may be overwhelmed with 'facts' about Asperger's, many of them inaccurate and even frightening. If you meet parents who are in this stage, the last thing they need to hear is how hard your life is in trying to deal with problems in the classroom. Be gentle and supportive. If you already know the

child, then mention every positive thing you can about her. Assure the parents that, together, you and they will create a great environment in which their child will thrive.

2. The parents may then go through denial. If you are trying to explain difficulties to parents in this stage, then it is quite likely they will simply tell you to be a better teacher as there is nothing wrong with their child. In this case, simply deal with each issue gently and calmly and do not refer to the diagnosis of Asperger's.

3. This is closely followed by anger and frustration. Someone or something has to be blamed for the child's diagnosis. The parents may barge into school and demand that unrealistic things be done for their child and they should be done *now*. Always listen to the angry parents and allow them to have their say. Understand that it is anger and frustration talking, and that the parent most likely has no ill feeling towards you. Keep calm and try to devise a plan that combines home and school to assist the child.

4. The parents may then slip into depression and guilt. They may blame themselves for the child's diagnosis and feel that they are useless parents. They may feel that their child has no real future and that things will only get worse. If you recognize that the parents are in this stage, do everything you can to highlight the positives of the child. Build up the child's self-esteem in class. If you have to talk to the parents about problems that have arisen, then make sure you stress positives first. Don't expect the parents to come up with a plan to solve the issue as they simply will not have the energy. Rather, have a plan in mind of how you want to deal with the situation and express real hope that things will be sorted soon.

5. Finally the parents will come to the realization that their child is not so bad after all. They start to see the real child rather than mourning a child they thought they had. They will start to laugh at anecdotes and be proud of successes and recognize the unique way of thinking as a good thing. These

parents will fight you like a lion protecting a cub if you do not come up to their expectations and do not support and protect their child. However, if you actively work with them and you do whatever it takes to teach their child then you will have a friend for life.

Manners

Manners matter. This is a fact of life that is true for everyone but is even more so for those with Asperger Syndrome. When a child does not automatically understand social expectations or pick up on communication clues, being able to fall back on good old-fashioned manners can be a lifeline. Manners are even more important when the child reaches an age where she seeks a job or starts to interact with adults on a daily basis. For many people, being 'normal' simply means knowing the manners expected in a situation and following them. A child does not have to 'read' a situation in order to shake hands with someone she is being introduced to or say good morning first thing in the morning. A child who eats with her mouth closed gets less attention than one who shovels in food and masticates for all to see. A peer might not care too much about pushing in a chair after getting up from a table, or holding a door open for others, but adults and prospective employers notice these things. For a child with Asperger's, not being noticed for the wrong reasons is just as important as being noticed for the right reasons.

Over and over again, adults on the spectrum (those who have an Autism Spectrum Disorder) who have written about their life experiences stress how manners have allowed them to be accepted in the 'normal' world and how simply applying manners opens doors when intelligence and aptitude without manners often fails.

Of course, good manners can benefit all your students, so take the time to instil, inform and expect good manners in your class. Make sure that you model these behaviours on a daily basis.

Some commonly accepted good manners are:

- Greet people appropriately when you meet. This might mean a high five to friends, a polite 'Good morning, sir' to the headmaster each time you see him and shaking your dad's boss's hand when he comes to visit.

- Say please, thank you, excuse me and sorry.
- If you can't say something nice, do not say anything at all.
- Do not interrupt when others are speaking.
- Do not comment negatively on other people's personal hygiene or looks.
- Hold the door open for others. Allow others, especially adults or people more senior or 'important' than you, to go through doors first.
- Knock on closed doors before entering.
- Let older people, or someone carrying something heavy, or pregnant ladies, have your seat on a bus or train.
- Push in your chair when you get up from a table.
- Cover your mouth when you cough or sneeze.
- Do not talk with your mouth full.
- Learn to use cutlery correctly.
- Introduce the friends you are with to the people you meet.
- Do not burp or pass wind in others' company. (There are exceptions when around mates.)
- When receiving gifts, thank the giver with a positive comment even if the gift is not liked.

Hygiene

Some children with Asperger's have difficulty with hygiene issues. Some do not like to shower or wash their hair or change their clothes. Younger children may unself-consciously pick their noses. They may not brush their teeth or comb their hair or wear deodorant. Frankly,

as a teacher there is not a lot you can do about these things. However, if you notice that they become an issue for your student or are causing the child to be isolated by others, it is worth having a quiet chat with the child and alerting the parents and caregivers to the problem.

Understanding why the child behaves in a certain way is important. Often the issue is a sensory one. The child with touch sensitivities may hate the feeling of water on her body and in fact may feel pain from water shooting from a nozzle. Toothbrushes can hurt gums and the taste of toothpaste may make the child gag. The smell of soaps and deodorants can be overwhelming and make the child physically ill. Some clothes are rough and scratchy on the child's skin so she sticks to the ones that are comfortable. A child with balance (vestibular) issues may be afraid of falling in the slippery shower and hates lowering her head to wash hair. Talk to the child and parent about all this and seek alternatives that the child can tolerate.

Sometimes the issue is one of priorities. The child simply does not see the need to groom properly when she could spend time on a special interest. Or it may be an issue of not being able to organize herself (executive functioning) to complete hygiene-related activities within a daily schedule.

The child also often does not make the link between good hygiene and making friends. She is not bothered by her own body odour and therefore does not understand that others avoid her because she smells. A teenage girl may not understand that, to be accepted by others, it is best she shaves her legs and underarms. A teenage boy might not realize that he is turning girls off by not trimming that straggly beard and brushing his hair. The younger child cannot comprehend that picking noses in public disturbs others.

All these issues can be discussed quietly with your student, parents and caregivers so a solution can be found. Your role as a teacher is to lead the classroom in treating the child with respect and dignity. *Never* berate or embarrass your student by pointing out hygiene issues publicly.

Educating the rest of the class

It is easy for your students to see that a child in a wheelchair cannot walk, and that those who are blind cannot see. It is not so easy to see or understand why someone with Asperger Syndrome behaves in certain ways. And the most important question here is, does your whole class need to know about the diagnosis of the Asperger child anyway?

If the child has obvious needs where she is taken from the room for extra help, or has a shadow teacher, or often displays unusual traits such as meltdowns and stimming (e.g. flapping hands, jumping on the spot, moving body), then naturally the other children will start to question why. It is important to have an explanation ready.

In many parts of the world, disabilities in any form are not talked about, or are hidden, or are a source of shame to the family. A child with a 'label' may be taunted by teachers and students alike. At other times, the parents may know of the diagnosis, but for very good reasons of their own have not told the child, or they do not want others to know about the diagnosis. In situations like this, it is most likely that you will be told of the child's diagnosis in confidence by the parents, or you simply believe from your own experience that your student falls within the spectrum. In those cases, it is vital that you as the classroom teacher keep that knowledge to yourself, all the while implementing every technique you can to help your student achieve her full potential.

Here are some things you can do:

- Explain to your class that everyone has strengths, weaknesses and needs, and each strength is to be valued and each weakness and need is to be understood and supported.

- Explain things such as stimming as simply how this child expresses happiness or fear or excitement. Be casual about it and the class will take your lead.

- If the child has a meltdown or is reacting badly to an overload of stimulation, be calm and in control, and say to the class 'It all got too much for Jimmy today. Let him calm down and I will talk to him later.'

- If other children ask why a child goes off for extra help or has a shadow teacher, say things like 'Everyone needs help in something that they are learning, and Jimmy needs help in English.'

- Build up an atmosphere of acceptance and support amongst your students and model it at every opportunity.

- Create a story where the main character has an Asperger trait that saves the day, for example: special interest knowledge solves a mystery; hypersensitive hearing overhears a plan for a robbery.

Where your student comes with the diagnosis and the parents and child are happy for others to know about it, then there are ways to help the rest of the class understand Asperger behaviours:

- In each chapter of this book there are classroom activities specially devised to explain a certain Asperger trait in a way that your other students can understand and empathize with.

- Read books to your class that explain Asperger Syndrome. See the References for some of these.

- Explain to the class ways in which they can help a fellow student with Asperger's. For example: invite them to play; if they look like they do not understand something, explain it to them; if they are acting 'weird' then try to understand why, rather than being upset or taunting them; if they are being socially unacceptable, gently point it out and help them understand what they did 'wrong'.

- Many sporting people and actors and businessmen are beginning to be open about their diagnosis. Invite a person with Asperger's who may have succeeded in some area to come and talk to the class.

At all times, present Asperger's as a different way of thinking and experiencing the world, and *not* as a defective way of being.

Organizing Your Student to be Organized

Executive Functioning

Description

Common complaints by teachers about their student with Asperger Syndrome are that the child loses things, does not get work in on time, does not follow directions, has to be told the same thing over and over, and cannot get himself organized. It is easy for the teacher to consider the child lazy, uncooperative, unmotivated and/or disobedient. Well, part of that is true. The 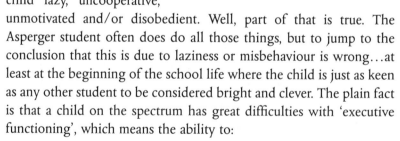 Asperger student often does do all those things, but to jump to the conclusion that this is due to laziness or misbehaviour is wrong…at least at the beginning of the school life where the child is just as keen as any other student to be considered bright and clever. The plain fact is that a child on the spectrum has great difficulties with 'executive functioning', which means the ability to:

- organize
- plan
- implement instructions

- problem-solve issues
- prioritize
- transition from one task to another
- multitask
- focus on tasks at hand
- self-monitor
- initiate and follow tasks through.

If these difficulties are not recognized and the child is not given the skills and support to address these issues, then naturally the child will flounder in the classroom. The more the child fails to 'obey' the teacher's commands to 'Finish your work!', 'Get the essay in on time!', 'Bring your things to school each day!' then the child's self-esteem crumbles and the child is even less able to perform to the teacher's standards. The teacher gets crosser and the situation spirals out of control until the child gives up and truly does becomes 'lazy' or 'unmotivated'. It is vital that you recognize your student's difficulties in executive functioning and support the child so that he can function as a valued and productive member of your classroom.

The child with difficulties in executive functioning:

- often loses books, notes and personal items
- often forgets to bring required items to school/sporting activities
- has difficulty with problem solving
- finds it difficult to create or initiate plans, to keep track of schedules and to organize others
- does not complete homework and assignments on time, if at all
- has difficulties getting dressed and ready for school each morning, or getting ready and changed for sporting activities at school
- seems to be the last one to know what is going on

- follows instructions at first but then forgets those instructions just a short time later

- does not have a system for sorting notes/items/belongings

- loses track of time

- finds it hard to relate newly learned material to previously learned material

- finds it hard to incorporate past knowledge into a discussion or assignment

- has difficulty remembering new information long enough to implement it; for example, can do new work in class but has forgotten how to do it by the time he gets home

- may pay attention to minor details but not see how they fit into a bigger picture

- finds it hard to do, or to think about, two or more things at once; can't multitask

- finds it hard to memorize something while actually doing it, for example remembering a number while phoning it

- gets very confused if given too many options

- goes along one track of thought or action and, even if it is wrong, will not seek help or change direction

- finds it hard to self-critique his own work and monitor his own progress and actions

- finds it very difficult to explain, verbally or in written form, a sequence of events either to instruct others how something should be done, or to explain a past event

- may make decisions impulsively without checking if it suits others

- may get very frustrated and upset when having to deal with orders and instructions imposed by others

- may repeat things over and over that only need to be done once, for example may sharpen a pencil many times in one lesson.

SEE ALSO

Adapting to Change

Homework

HOW YOUR STUDENT MAY EXPLAIN IT

☼ I would rather not go to a party if it meant I had to work out what clothes to wear, what present to buy and how to get there. Those things are enormous problems for me. Huge. I freeze and don't know where to start.

☼ I would rather not eat if it meant I had to make my own lunch. What should I eat? Should I have leftovers, or make a sandwich? If leftovers, which bowl do I use in the microwave? How long should I heat it for? If a sandwich, which bread, brown or white, and which filling? Meat? Cheese? Spread? The choices are too many. I stand at the fridge too long. I close the door and go back on the computer.

☼ My head is full of information, but if I'm put on the spot, everything goes blank. If I try to talk to people, I have to stop and search for the right word and I look stupid. Teachers ask me things I know and then suddenly the answer is gone. I know the answer ten minutes later.

☀ I try to remember things. I take notes and then lose them. I remember the letters in a mnemonic, but not what they stand for. I learn very quickly at school, then forget things by the time I get home. It is so frustrating that I scream inside my head. Why can't I remember like other people? How hard can it be? But I can't. I just can't. And yelling at me, telling me I can, doesn't change a thing.

At school

The first thing you can do for your Asperger student is to acknowledge that he has legitimate difficulties with executive functioning and then give assistance and support rather than complaints and punishment. Once you realize that the child actually wants to succeed, is intelligent enough to succeed and, with help, has a good chance of succeeding, then there are many things you can do in the classroom to support and encourage the child and promote success.

One thing to remember is that giving the child *knowledge* on how to be more organized does not actually help very much. Over the years, he has most likely been inundated with knowledge. It is taped inside his homework diaries and plastered on the bedroom door and hung on the fridge with bright magnets. Quite possibly the child can even recite things such as: read the question, highlight the important information, write your answer, check your work for spelling and grammar mistakes. Or perhaps the list is how to get ready each morning at home and includes things such as: make your bed, pack your school bag, eat breakfast. However, the practicalities of each step can be quite beyond the child's ability to understand and follow. He may ask 'What are important bits to highlight?', 'What do I pack in my school bag?'

Take the time to model the things you wish the child to do. If you want the child to get out the text book and open it to page 12, then get out *your* text book and open it to page 12 and show the class what page 12 looks like. If you want the child to get his things and come with you, then be specific, and say 'Get the books on your desk, put them in your school bag, then bring your bag and come with me.'

Here are some other important things you can do to help:

- Children on the spectrum are usually visual learners and appreciate concrete reminders of what they need to be doing. Make your lessons as visual as possible, using graphs, charts, lists, timelines, and so on. Write instructions on the board. Hand out To-Do lists. Use pictures on calendars to inform of upcoming events such as concerts or sports days. Give age-appropriate visual instructions of common activities. Sometimes even children in upper grades can benefit from picture clues about things that are coming up next.

- When giving assignments, sit with the child and map out a schedule for getting the work completed. Break it up into small, easily completed sections, highlight in colour the important bits, set a date for the completion of each section and mark each section as it is done. This avoids the situation where the child is trying desperately to complete a month of work the night before it is due.

- Homework diaries that go between teacher and parent are essential. Make sure the child has it updated before he leaves the class, and encourage the parent to make sure it is brought back to school the next day. Help the child mark in all dates for homework, assignments, exams, sporting activities, and so on.

- Allow a trustworthy child in the class to help your Asperger student keep up with the class work. Rather than having to ask the teacher all the time what he has to do, the child has permission to talk to the 'helper' to be reminded which number activity has to be completed, or what he has to do next.

- Write instructions on the board or hand out information sheets, and do not force your students to rely on remembering your verbal instructions.

- Use mnemonics and acronyms and acrostics to help the child remember things. For example, My Very Easy Memory Jingle Saves Us Naming Planets can be used to recall the order of the planets – Mercury, Venus, Earth, Mars, Jupiter, Saturn, Uranus, Neptune, Pluto. (Well, at least it could when Pluto was still classed as a planet!)

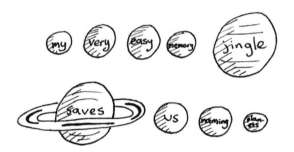

- Even if your student is in an upper grade, do not presume that he knows how to write an essay, how to complete an assignment or how to present work properly. Take the time to explain to your class exactly what you want done. Write out your expectations on a hand-out sheet. Clearly show how the work will be graded.

- It may be appropriate for you to shorten assignments or reduce homework expectations (see **Homework**). This is not done to show favouritism to the child, but rather to acknowledge the disability the child has in this area. It also recognizes that the amount of effort and concentration the child with Asperger's has to put into a project is way more than that of his peers.

- Most school-wide testing programmes acknowledge the need for certain students to be given extra help in exams. Check if your students are eligible for this type of assistance. Help may include: extra time; doing the test on a computer; allowing a reader to come into the exam and read each question aloud to the student; and allowing the student to answer exam questions verbally while another person writes his answer.

- When explaining an essay or an assignment to your student, tape your conversation on his phone or on a recording device. This way the child can replay it later and parents can also listen to what is expected.

- Allow the child to sit in a place in the classroom where there are fewest distractions. This might be at the end of the row, or the front of the class, or at a side desk. Never isolate the child in a way that he feels punished.

- Allow the child to put on the desk only items that are relevant to the subject being taught.

- Minimize clutter in your classroom to help prevent the child being distracted by irrelevant items.

- Be aware of sensory input that may distract the child, for example fluorescent lights, sounds next door, canteen smells (see **Sensory Issues**).

- Distortion of time is a major problem for a child with executive functioning issues. Things he loves seem to take minutes and then the lesson is over and he does not want to move to the next subject. Things he hates feel like they drag forever. This is true for all students of course…and teachers! However, if the child thinks that doing a task he hates will last forever, and therefore does not even want to start, break the task into small time slots. Instead of setting the task of completing maths sums on pages 8, 9 and 10, say 'I will give you five minutes to finish five sums… Go!' To give an even greater incentive then add 'The more sums you do, the less homework I will give.' Every child can cope with five minutes of a hated task. Correct the work so the children all know they are doing the sums correctly, then go on to the next five. Suddenly the child will have completed all the sums whereas, if left to his own efforts, would not have had the incentive or ability to regulate his time to complete half the sums.

Classroom activity

- To help your students have an understanding of how time can feel longer or shorter according to how much enjoyment they are having, do a variety of activities and have the children guess how long the activity took. Get them to chart the results.

Activity	How long I thought it took	How long it really took
Stand on one foot with eyes closed		
Write the alphabet with the non-dominant hand		
Watch a funny YouTube clip		

Home link

- Discuss with parents and caregivers the things you are doing in the classroom to help the child with executive functioning. Go over the hints and ideas in the **Home link** in **Homework**. Help them understand that to demand that the child gets ready, or does things on time, is not helpful to the child. The child needs to be shown, perhaps many times, how to pack a school bag, how to get dressed in the morning, and so on.

- Suggest that the parent times the child as he does chores and school work at home. The child might be amazed that emptying the dishwasher can be done in three minutes. Help the child understand that often things seem to take a long time, but in fact can be done quite quickly. This is a surprisingly simple but effective technique to help the child organize himself.

- Suggest that the parent makes picture charts to show the steps needed to be organized. For example, how to get ready for bed.

Brush your teeth	Have a shower	Get into your pyjamas	Get into bed
			You can now read for 15 minutes

- Suggest that the parent and child draw up a chart with two columns. 'To Do' and 'Done'. On the To Do side, write a list of all the tasks the child has to do in one day. At first include everything: get out of bed, make bed, get dressed, make breakfast, eat breakfast, brush teeth, brush hair, and so on. At the end of the day, things included might be: do sums on page 3, write intro for history essay, half an hour piano practice, walk dog. Then as the child does an activity, cross it off, and write it on the Done side. Help the child understand that the things do not have to be completed in order. As the Done side starts to fill up, the child can get a feeling for how the day is mapped out and can feel satisfied at all the things he manages to do in one day.

Adapting to Change

Description

People with Asperger Syndrome often find it hard to adapt to change. There are two main reasons for this:

1. They get satisfaction and comfort in sameness and don't like to change. It is important to understand how confusing life can be when a person has to juggle and cope with an overwhelming influx of sights, sounds, smells, tastes, interactions and expectations. Keeping to routine, and knowing what will come next, brings a structure, purpose and order to the day and helps calm the anxiety and fear that threatens to overload the person with Asperger's on a daily basis.

2. They are fixated on a rule or mindset and find it hard to break it. Some rules and mindsets are obvious, like 'only cross the road at the traffic light'. The child may then find it almost impossible to cross a road that does not have a traffic light. Other rules and mindsets can come about indirectly from one-off comments or overheard conversations or misunderstanding of words. A child who has heard that a boy's voice has broken, that is, has become deeper with puberty, may live in fear that his own voice will 'break' and therefore tries to avoid this own change in his voice.

The child:

- prefers when things are clear, regular and unchanged

- may find it hard to move from one activity to the next in a normal daily programme, especially if she had not completed the tasks for the first activity

- needs warning signals that an activity is about to come to an end; for example, 'In five minutes, you will need to pack away your books'

- can concentrate intensely for a very long time on an activity she enjoys

- may be unwilling to try new things for fear of not doing them well

- may resist doing something that she has previously understood to be forbidden or dangerous, for example go into an out-of-bounds area, even with teacher presence and permission

- is a stickler for rules and often acts like the class policeman

- may have strong preference for certain foods (limited diet), clothing (likes to wear the same thing day after day), toys (plays with the same thing over and over), and so on

- may insist that routines are followed exactly every day to the tiniest details and gets upset if the routine is broken

- gets upset with ambiguous situations and needs to know definites; for example, gets distressed if the family *might* go to the beach tomorrow

- may have ritualistic conversations daily where the other person must answer the same way each time; for example, must say 'Goodnight, I love you' three times every night before sleeping and can't sleep until this is said

- may have compulsive behaviour where a routine must be followed before the next thing can happen; for example, may want the light switched on and off three times before sleeping, or must hop on every second tile before entering a room

- enjoys mundane activities such as lining up objects in a row or sharpening pencils, and can keep up this activity for a very long period of time without showing signs of boredom

- is happy to watch the same video or show over and over again

- may have an amazing memory for things other people quickly forget; for example, remembering the seating positions of everyone at last year's party

- may have an amazing memory of her own childhood, recalling things from early years and even months of life

- may have a photographic memory

- finds it hard to apply something learned to a new situation

- does not like to do something if there is a possibility of failure

- may pursue a line of thinking that is wrong rather than changing her ways.

SEE ALSO

Preparing for Your Student with Asperger Syndrome

Preparing yourself and the classroom

Before the start of the school year

Hints for parents to prepare the child for the new school year

Field Trips, Excursions and Camps

HOW YOUR STUDENT MAY EXPLAIN IT

When I am doing something I like, it takes over my mind and I put all my effort and energy into it. I am in a different world and it makes me happy and I feel calm and excited at the same time.

Then if my 'world' is snatched out of my hand, or my computer is switched off, or I have someone suddenly put their face close to mine and yell that I have to stop what I am doing, then it is terrifying and confusing. I need time to move out of my own zone or I can't cope. I just need time. And no yelling.

- Even at the mention of something new, I panic. I feel numb and desperate. Even after the new thing happens, the feelings don't go away and can stay for months. I wish I wasn't this way, but I am.
- The beginning of every term, every year is the same. I get new schedules, new classes, new teachers, new rooms. Even if I go to the same old room, I get lost even after being at the same school for years. And it's not even a big school. I am always late to class because I go to the wrong room, or I forget which books to take and have to go back to my locker to get them. So for the first few weeks of every term I am useless and lost. I spend a lot of time in the toilet where I can panic in peace.
- I want Mum to drive me to school at 60km/hr because that is the speed limit. I hate it when she goes faster because then she is breaking the rule. But I also hate it when she goes slower, because the sign says 60km/hr so that is the speed she should do. If other people are in the way and make us go slower, then I feel wrong. I think 60km/hr should be 60km/hr and that is that.

At school

One of the most important things a teacher can do for a child who dislikes change is not to create an environment without change, but rather give the child coping skills for when things do change. The first step, however, is to create a regular routine and a safe place for the student and then bring in changes slowly while helping the child to adjust. When it comes to a child's adherence to rules, this can be a great thing, and something to be praised. However, make sure that rigid and blind following of rules does not become detrimental in any way. Teach the child that there are times when a rule might need to be broken; for example, if there is a fire she might need to go to an out-of-bounds area.

Here are some things you can do to help the child cope with change:

- Remember how important routine is to a child with Asperger's. It helps her make sense of the world around her. Simply allowing the child to sit in the same chair each day can calm and orientate her. By you adhering to the day's schedule, the child is not jerked out of her comfort zone and is more likely to settle and complete the tasks at hand.

- If a child asks the same question over and over, for example 'What time is lunch-time?', then make up a card with a visual answer such as a clock with 1pm on it with a person eating. Then when the child asks the question, point to the answer.

- Many children with Asperger Syndrome are visual learners and cope best with change when they can see or read instructions and programmes rather than just hear them. Use as many visual supports as possible. Write instructions on the board. Hand out To-Do lists. Use pictures on calendars to inform of upcoming events such as concerts or sports days. Give age-appropriate visual instructions of common activities. Sometimes even children in upper grades can benefit from picture clues about things that are coming up next.

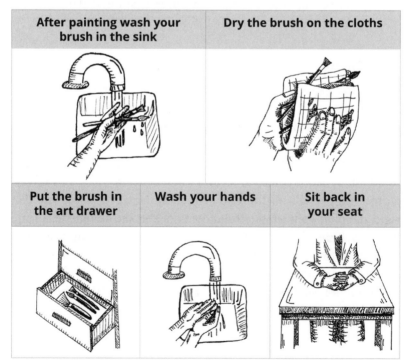

- If the student ignores your instructions, such as, 'Finish one task and go to the next', do not presume she is being disobedient or 'not adapting to change' again. It is quite possible that the child is so engrossed in the task that your request was simply not heard. Or perhaps it has not even registered that all the other children are now doing something different. Gently get the child's attention and repeat your instruction, and even better, give a time warning so the child can move her thoughts away from the task at hand. It is much better to allow the child a few minutes more to be mentally ready to change, than to force a change and have her unsettled for hours.

- The child may need more input from you than your other students do to keep her on track. Sometimes all that is needed is a quick prompting or a simple re-explanation of the task. Sometimes the child will need extra time to complete the work. Some children with Asperger's benefit greatly from a shadow teacher or classroom assistant to help with keeping her on task and helping with classroom routines.

- Where possible, write the day's schedule on the board or on a chart. This is especially important if a change is made to the day's routine, such as having a visiting guest, or fire drill. Where possible keep to this schedule or give good warning if the schedule needs to change.

- Send weekly planners home so the caregivers can help the child prepare for the next day's lessons and activities.

- Prepare age-appropriate warnings that the lesson is about to end. For younger children, perhaps sing a clean-up song. For older children, ring a bell, or simply use a consistent clear instruction: 'In five minutes we will close our books.' Avoid general terms such as, 'Almost finished, everyone?'

- If a child has to move from one room to the next for different subjects, this can cause anxiety, especially if it is early in the term when the routine is new, or if it is an unexpected change. For the first few times, go with the child, or organize a helper or friend to watch out for her. Regardless of the child's age, explain *exactly* what will happen. Many children resist change simply because they do not know what to do next. Some children dawdle to class for the same reason. Many children express great relief to have the 'next steps' explained in great detail: 'When the first class finishes, pack all your books into your school bag. Then walk along this corridor and turn right and go to the class marked "Miss Smith". Go inside. Take out your English book and your pens. Check in your diary to see if you had any homework for that day. If so, open your books to show your homework.'

- Most children with Asperger's do not appreciate surprises, even ones that should be pleasurable. For instance, if the child loves dinosaurs and you have a palaeontologist guest speaker come to the class, do not expect the child to be happy if you announce suddenly, 'Instead of today's art lesson, we have a special visitor.' The child will be more likely to focus on the fact that the schedule has been unexpectedly changed, and she already has her art things out and was mentally ready to paint. Therefore she will not express any joy at the thought of listening to someone speak on her favourite topic. It would be even worse if she was forced unexpectedly to give up her favourite subject, such as computer class, for a demonstration from, say, a famous basketball player.

- If there is more than one teacher or adult in the room, then be sure that only one gives instructions for a given project. Too many voices and instructions can be confusing.

- Relief or substitute teachers constitute a major change in the child's routine. Some caregivers with children with Asperger's even prefer to keep their child home on the day the class teacher is absent as the disruption to the child is so great that it can take days to get over it. Obviously this is not something that can be condoned all throughout the child's schooling years. It is better to teach the child coping strategies than to let her avoid stressful situations. If possible, get the same relief teacher each time so the child can build up a relationship and understanding with this teacher. Notify the caregiver *before* the child arrives at school that the teacher will be absent, so that the child will not get an unwelcome surprise when arriving at class.

With school and caregiver permission, write up a student profile outlining the child's traits, strengths, weaknesses, and any other important information so the relief teacher knows the best way to deal with issues that may arise. Be sure to give both the relief teacher and the child a way of getting outside help if things go wrong. If the school has an intercom system, then leave the intercom number for the school counsellor or relevant adult who can be called if the child has a tantrum or meltdown. Have a safe place in the classroom where the child can go if the stress is getting too much for her and be sure the relief teacher knows all about this process.

- Help the child to help herself. In most cases, the child is unable to prevent changes to schedules or prevent unexpected events from happening. Lead the child to understand that things will often happen that are out of her control. However, the child *can* be in control of her own reactions. Teach the child to say things like, 'Sorry, I didn't hear you. Can you please tell me again what you want me to do?', 'Can I please have five more minutes so I can finish this work?' or 'I have missed the bus. Can you please help me?'

- Be aware that physical changes in the classroom can bring great anxiety to your student. Never rearrange furniture overnight so that the child is seated differently the next day. Rather, if moving the furniture is necessary or desirable, have the class help so that before the children leave school that day, they know where they will sit the next day. If you wish to put up a display of art work, or change your posters, then get the child to help you. That way she is in some degree of control of the change.

- At the beginning of the school year, and perhaps even at the beginning of each term, allow the child and the caregiver to come to your class a few days before school starts to orientate herself. Show the child where she will be sitting and where to place her school bag and books. Give a tour of the school, even if the child has been there before. Show eating areas, play areas, library, and so on. Give the child a map of the school and show the areas where she will mostly frequent and which parts are out of bounds. Be sure to use words carefully and do not say 'You are not allowed to go to these areas', or the child will never go to those areas in any situation. Say, rather, that these areas are only for special times and the teachers will let you know when you can go there.

- When introducing a new topic or activity, understand that the child may resist learning simply because it is new and scary, not because the child is bored or incapable of learning. If possible, spend a little one-on-one time with the child before the lesson. If you are introducing baseball, for example, then at lunch-time the day before, get the child to help you bring the equipment from the sports room. Show the child how to hold the bat and let her hit the ball a few times. Then on the day of the lesson, ask the child to show others how to hold the bat. This will build up self-esteem and confidence. Remember that many children (and not only those with Asperger's) learn best with a big-picture approach. Explain to the class the entire game of baseball, the basic rules, who stands where, why they have to hit the ball, why the fielder has to pick up the ball and throw it back to base as fast as possible, and so on. Only then, ask the children to practise throwing a ball to each other. When there is a reason for learning something new, then the child is much more likely to participate.

- If a child has developed an adherence to a 'rule' that is overtaking her life, or causing other issues, then this must be discussed so the child sees the reason for breaking rules at times. For example, a child may have heard that carbohydrates are bad for the health and therefore tries to cut all carbohydrates out of her diet. Or the child was told to chew her food twenty times before swallowing and does so meticulously, counting each chew, making her the last to finish eating at meal-times and an object of ridicule with peers. Use logic and facts to show that there are times that 'rules' are not rules, but guidelines for safety and health.

- Sometimes a child with Asperger's will become the class 'policeman' and insist that everyone, child and adult alike, obeys every rule to the letter. Gently explain that although it is great to follow the rules, the child is not in charge of other children or adults. Do not allow any children to use rules to bully or belittle each other.

- Sometimes the child will conform and perform better if she understands that she is obeying a rule. If the rule is written down, even better. Then, when there is a struggle to get the child to obey or behave in a certain way, bring out the rule book and show the child the rule. This also helps the child to understand that the teacher is not being 'mean' by insisting on something, but that the teacher, too, is obeying rules.

- The child thinks in cause-and-effect and can hold to this view rigidly even when the effect changes. For example, if one day the child comes up to you while you are on playground duty, and you chat happily until class time, it is very likely the child will believe this is now a pattern that will go on forever. The child will be upset and confused if, the next time you are on duty, you suggest she goes off to play. If you can see that your actions (i.e. talking to the child the first time) led the child to a misconception of how you will behave every time from then onwards, take the time to explain how situations can change from day to day. Explain that you are there on duty for all children, not just one child, and that other children want to talk to you too. Help the child investigate other ways of spending lunch-time. It may even help if the child has a schedule for which day she can spend time chatting with you on duty. However, if you agree that Monday is your chat day, then keep to it as rigidly as possible or you will then have to deal with an extremely unsettled child for the rest of that day.

- In extreme situations where the child is incapable of adapting, it may be necessary to seek extra help and advice from medical specialists.

Classroom activity

- Discuss with the class what it would feel like if you were doing something very enjoyable and then suddenly were whisked away to a different place or world where nothing made sense. Have the children write a story describing what happened and how they felt.

    If appropriate, and with caregiver permission, explain how a child with Asperger's feels like this each time she is forced to do something or go somewhere when she is not ready or prepared for it.

Home link

- Work with the caregivers to help the child learn techniques to adapt to change. For example, one child had a serious meltdown every time he missed the school bus home. The school and mother devised a plan. The teacher arranged to keep him busy after school long enough so that he would miss the bus. The bus monitor was pre-warned that the child would have a meltdown when he realized the bus had already gone. The teacher was ready to come to him and help him to call his mother to let her know he needed to be picked up that day. The mother came promptly and praised her son for calling her. When he settled, the teacher and mother sat with him and went through the steps of what to do if the bus leaves without him. It did not take long for this in itself to become a routine and soon the child no longer panicked if he missed the bus.

- Keep a class diary for the parent or caregiver to write in if they wish to convey relevant information on various matters to the teacher. For instance, the caregiver may warn the teacher that a pet had died the night before, or a teacher may warn the caregiver that he will be away the next day at a conference. The teacher can also write homework expectations such as, 'The English sentence work should take no longer than ten minutes.' That way the parent knows that the child has a problem if she is still unfinished after half an hour.

- Explain to the caregivers that the child will work best with a routine. If there is a set time and place and time limit given to homework, the child is more likely to complete it within that time. If there is a set bedtime every night, then the child is less likely to argue about going to bed. Having some sort of sensory link to the routine can also help. Dim the lights or light a scented candle five minutes before bedtime. Put on some calm music and have the TV and computer screen off while doing homework.

Understanding the Perspectives of Others

Theory of Mind

Description

Theory of Mind, or mind blindness, is a much-bandied-around term when it comes to Asperger Syndrome. In its simplest terms it means that those on the autism spectrum find it very difficult to understand that other people think differently from them and that other people have their own ideas, beliefs, wants, desires and points of view. Or perhaps, more correctly, those with Asperger's may understand that others think differently from them, but how and why and what others think is a complete mystery to them. They find it hard to put themselves in 'other people's shoes', to empathize in a way others expect, and can find people's actions bewildering and unpredictable and frightening.

Some people on the spectrum say that rather than being mind *blind*, they are actually able to see the possibilities of so many ways a person may react, and they absorb so much information about a social situation, that they become paralysed by all the input. It is like having no filters for incoming information, and due to the bombardment on their thoughts and senses they in effect close down and react woodenly or in a monotone, giving the impression they are uninterested or do not understand.

Whatever the reason, difficulties with Theory of Mind affects every part of the child's life, from forming friendships, to being able to navigate social norms, to understanding what others are thinking and feeling. It also affects how a child may show emotions and helps explain why a child thinks and speaks the way he does.

The child:

- is very egocentric (not to be confused with egotistic)

- uses logic rather than intuition in social situations

- has great difficulty understanding that other people have different views and wants and desires from him

- will presume that other people love or dislike and want the same things as he does

- may start talking to a person about an incident, but start in the middle of the story presuming the person knows the beginning

- may walk away from others presuming they will follow or know that he is leaving

- may talk about a special interest oblivious to the fact that he is boring the listener

- may interrupt conversations without considering how this affects those who are talking

- may try to barge in to other people's games or activities without realizing it will upset them

- tries to control games and activities his way

- may be rigid in thinking and will not change his opinions or stance easily

- sees things in 'black and white'

- may find it difficult to separate fact from fiction

- may find it very difficult to apologize or to see his fault in a confrontation or see the need for an apology

- may say what he is thinking without considering others' feelings

- may criticize or correct others, thinking he is helping that person; however, comes across as rude or arrogant

- will often offend people or get into trouble and have no idea why

- may not be able to discern the motives behind others' actions and can over- or under-react to provocation; for example, may hit a person who accidently bumps him thinking it was an attack, or may not get upset when a bully smacks him on the back thinking it is a form of friendship

- may not understand the difference between someone hurting him unintentionally or intentionally and react as if the action was intentional

- tends to take a literal interpretation of what others say

- may be considered rude or naughty when he does not obey social rules

- may be considered unemotional or to have no empathy when he does not pick up on the signals that others are hurt or need comfort

- is very honest, even at times when honesty can be considered rude or embarrassing

- may be socially isolated as he does not conform to the way others expect him to behave

- does not pick up on non-verbal clues or understand sarcasm or other inflections in the voice

- may trust that if other people want their feelings and thoughts known they will clearly say so

- cannot comprehend why a person would try to convey a message or emotion with vague gestures or hints when he could speak clearly with words

- may choose to avoid social situations where his actions may be misunderstood

- after spending time in social situations, may be physically and emotionally exhausted from the effort of trying to read social and non-verbal cues.

SEE ALSO

Literal Thinkers And Speakers

Forming Friendships and Following Social Rules

Apparent Lack of Emotions

Bullying

HOW YOUR STUDENT MAY EXPLAIN IT

꙳ I have come to understand that other people think and speak and react differently from me. But most people don't bother to try to understand why I think and speak and react differently from them. Why am I the one who has to change? If Aspies were the majority then people everywhere would behave logically and say what they mean. Wouldn't that be great!

꙳ I often have no idea what other people are thinking or why they do the things they do. It's like there is a huge crevasse between me and them. I see their faces screw up and they do weird things with their body parts, and then they expect something from me and I am the one who gets into trouble if I don't miraculously understand what is expected of me. Most of the time I am afraid of people, so stay away from them if I can.

꙳ I get surprised all the time. I am surprised when people don't like the things I like. I am surprised when people do not know the things that I know and I am surprised that people know things that I don't know. I am surprised that people expect me to understand how they feel and what they are thinking. How is that possible? I am not them.

At school

The child with Asperger's, with his lack of Theory of Mind, is a prime target in schools for being bullied, being socially ostracized, and is often accused of being rude or disobedient. Beware of this, and promote a classroom environment of acceptance and understanding, and at all times be as fair and open-minded as possible when dealing with difficulties that may arise on a day-to-day basis for your Asperger student.

Here are some ways you can help:

- It is very likely that your student with Asperger's will start to tell you something without giving any background. For example, he may say 'Sally fell down and cried and cried.' Gently stop the child and remind him that you do not understand what he is talking about. Is someone hurt and needing help? Is this a movie plot? Was it something that happened at home or happened a long time ago? Insist that the child goes back and fills in the details. The child may get frustrated but it is very important that he understands that you do not have the same knowledge that he has.

- All children want to be respected and valued and have others recognize their accomplishments. Children with Asperger's may not understand how giving compliments to others can make them feel good about themselves and can open doors to friendship. Encourage the use of compliments in your classroom and be generous with your own giving of compliments. Be specific with your praise. Don't say 'Great work', but rather, 'You painted that tree extremely realistically. Well done.' Praise your students when they compliment each other. Explain how to take compliments well; for example, if someone says 'Your painting is great', the correct response is 'Thanks', not 'The colour is all wrong. I hate this painting.'

- When there is a conflict in the classroom, be very careful to listen to both sides of the story. Let the child with Asperger's speak first as, at first, he will only be able to see his side of the story. Allow no interruptions. ('Jimmy took my toy so I hit him.') Then let the second child speak, again allowing no one to interrupt. ('I picked up the toy but I didn't know it was Jenny's and she hit me.') The child with Asperger's gets two important things from this. He will soon trust you and know that you will be fair and listen to what he says. The child will also learn that the other child has a different point of view. You are then free to give your own interpretation of what you saw, or if you didn't see the incident, then explain the steps in coming to some solutions. ('I am the teacher and I can't let my students hurt each other. See the rule on the board – No hitting. Jenny, you must sit on the quiet seat for five minutes. Next time someone takes your toy, then ask for it back politely, or you may choose to share next time.') Of course, it is quite possible that Jimmy knew full well that it was Jenny's toy and took it to annoy her. Be very wary of this side of your students, and if necessary get a third, unbiased, side of the story. (Or take mind-reading lessons, which could help you resolve all your class conflicts ever after!)

- Try to help the child understand that everyone has a reason for doing what they do. Let the child understand that you know he often gets confused by the things other people do. However, explain that the child also does things that are confusing to you and to the other students. Promote an environment where your students ask each other, 'Why did you do that?' before they get angry or react. Reinforce this when you go into conflict resolutions. Make each child ask the other 'Why did you do that?' and make them repeat the answer back to you. 'Jenny said that she hit me because I took her toy.'

- If a child with Asperger's breaks a rule, always explain clearly what he has done wrong and why a punishment is needed. Most often he will have no idea why he is in trouble. Be very specific. It makes things easier if consequences for misbehaviours are already written down and made clear to the class. Make sure you listen to why the child broke the rule as it may be for a very different reason than you thought. Help the child transfer an understanding of the rule to different situations; for example, 'Don't scribble on classroom walls' means also not scribbling on playground walls and toilet walls.

- Use social stories, or draw cartoon pictures, to help the child see all sides of a conflict. Help the child see that the other students have thoughts and feelings too and they are not always the same as the child's. Show that ignoring the feelings and wants of others may cause them to react in an angry way. Cause and effect. (See **Body Language Blindness**.)

- Be wary of trying to help a child with Asperger's understand how to behave around others by saying 'Do unto others, what you want done unto you.' It may help him see that other people do not like to be hit or hurt or made fun of, but the child's perspective of what he wants 'done unto them' could be very different from others in certain situations. For example, the Asperger child may like to be left alone when sad or troubled, so leaves others alone when they are sad or troubled. The child may not like to be touched, so does not touch others. He may like it when others speak the honest truth and so he speaks the honest truth. By stressing that to treat others in the way they like to be treated could actually harm his ability to relate to others.

- Promote an environment where the child feels comfortable coming to you to ask questions and seek clarification on things he does not understand.

Classroom activities

- Have children imagine that they are dignitaries at an international conference and that they represent a fictional country. Give them a card each with the norms and rules of their country and things that would be insulting to them. Be as imaginative as you can and cover as many social customs as you can think of. Alternatively, get the children to make up the cards as a classroom activity in itself.

Example 1: Frownland	Example 2: Giggleville
Normal behaviour	*Normal behaviour*
• It is polite to frown at people • You must stare hard into people's eyes to get their respect • If people ask what you do, or where you come from, you must answer in as few words as possible • Stand as still as you can and do not fidget	• Giggle at everything • Use hands a lot when talking • Give very long answers to every little question • Hug people when you meet
Things that cause offence	*Things that cause offence*
• Smiling people, because they can't be trusted • Not looking into your eyes when you talk • Casual conversations about nothing much • People who use their hands to speak	• Frowning people, because they can't be trusted • People that stand stiffly when talking • Abrupt answers to questions

Now give out a card to each child and act out a social gathering at the conference. Then talk about how some people were insulted by other people's genuine attempts at friendliness. Note how people with the same cards tended to gather together by the end of a set time. Help them see that different people show their emotions and react in social settings in different ways and that these different behaviours are not wrong, just different. Discuss how an understanding of another person's customs can ease an awkward situation.

- Tell the story about three blindfolded men being allowed to touch an elephant for the first time. One man touched its side and thought that an elephant must be shaped like a wall. One touched its tail and thought it must be like a rope. The last blindfolded man touched its trunk and thought an elephant must look like a fat hose. Explain how everyone sees things a little differently depending on the information given. If allowed, explain that Asperger's is a bit like only seeing one part of the elephant.

- Paint a box different colours on all sides. Hold up the box in the middle of the classroom and ask the children what colour they see. Rotate the box and they call out the different colours from their perspective. Again this can show how we all see things in different ways depending on what angle we see them from.

- Role-play or write cartoon stories about an incident from the different viewpoints of those involved; for example, two children fighting and the teacher only sees the first child hit the second child, but not see that the second child had stolen the other child's hat. Write/draw about how each person sees things in a different way.

Home link

- Explain to the carers the steps you are taking in the class to assist the child in understanding other people's perspectives, thoughts and emotions. In turn, discuss how they deal with this at home. Try to be consistent with your approaches in the home and in the classroom so the child has positive behaviours reinforced and negative behaviours are dealt with consistently.

- Encourage the carers to put their thoughts, emotions and feelings into words so the child is clear about what is expected of him and does not have to guess what the carer is feeling or wanting.

- Encourage the carers to educate family members, friends and other people in the child's life about the child's mind blindness. Explain the techniques you use with your students to help them understand why the child acts and behaves in the way he does. Break down barriers so the child is accepted for who he is and supported when help is needed.

Body Language Blindness

Description

If a child was blind, and bumped into someone or tripped over, people would understand and rush to help. When a child is body language blind, her problems are not so easily understood or assisted. She finds it very difficult to know when someone is happy or angry; crying or laughing; wants to see her or wants her to go away. The child is likely to barge uninvited into others' social circles, talk over others' conversations, ignore 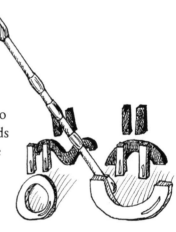 all the cues that her presence or conversation is unwanted, and perhaps most sad of all, may not realize when her presence is actually sought after and welcomed.

The child:

- may not alter behaviours for different situations; for example, may talk to a headteacher in the same way as to a peer

- can misinterpret a casual smile as an invitation to deeper friendship

- can misinterpret a smile of genuine friendship and believe she has no friends

- may find it hard to take turns in conversations and games as she does not pick up the hints that her turn is over

- can be bullied

- may have limited facial expressions and can be called a poker-face or robot

- may walk and move in an awkward way

- avoids direct eye contact with others

- may not understand the notion of personal space and stands too close to others

- may hate her own personal space being invaded

- may find it hard to recognize a person out of context, for example may not recognize a teacher when down at the beach (this has a name all of its own – *prosopagnosia*, or face blindness)

- can find it difficult to identify and describe emotions and can be accused of having no emotions at all as she may not react physically in a way others expect; for example, may not outwardly show sadness at news of a death (this too has its own name – *alexithymia*)

- can learn to read body language and facial expressions which can help alleviate many of the social problems she may encounter.

HOW YOUR STUDENT MAY EXPLAIN IT

💡 I just don't understand why I have to look someone in the eyes when they talk. It feels icky and makes me sick inside. Besides, I know what they look like and I can hear perfectly well without looking at their eyes. I wish I lived in one of those countries where looking at people's eyes is considered rude. I would be considered very polite there!

💡 It doesn't make sense that people can't just say what they mean. Why is it up to me to work out what they want or how they feel by thinking about where their arms are, how tight their mouth is, how many frown lines they are showing. It's stupid. We can all talk. We have voices and brains. Just say what you mean and life would be so much simpler.

At school

The old adage 'It takes a village to rear a child' is very appropriate for a child with Asperger's in a school environment. There are many adults with whom the child will come in contact; from the teachers, of course, to the helper at the front desk, to the librarian (who will probably see quite a bit of a child), to the classroom assistants, relief teachers and even the cleaners. With the parents' permission, inform other adults in the school about the child's Asperger traits. That way if she behaves in ways that seem unusual or too familiar, then they will realize it is not from cheekiness or rudeness. They will also be more aware of how to help her if she gets into difficulties outside the classroom.

Here are some ways you can help:

- A child with Asperger's is age, social status and sex blind. She will treat a four-year-old girl in much the same way she would treat an authoritarian headteacher. But she can learn that certain things are fine in one situation but inappropriate in another. If the adults around her are aware of this, then instead of yelling, they will know to remind the child gently that it is not okay to tell a visiting dignitary all about the mating habits of the Bolivian black beetle.

- Often a child with Asperger's will be ostracized by her peers for barging into their social circles uninvited or for interrupting their conversations with topics that don't interest them. If you see this happening, then take the child aside and explain the social faux pas. Help the child recognize the body language of her peers to see if her intrusions are welcome. Try to team up the child with another child with similar interests, or encourage a kind child in the class to befriend the child with Asperger's. (See **Forming Friendships and Following Social Rules**.)

- When a child has a problem due to misreading body language, draw cartoon pictures depicting the sequence of events to help the child see where she went wrong.

Two friends were holding hands and talking with heads close together.	You pushed between them and talked about computers.	One of them punched you.	You punched back harder.
The way they were standing showed they wanted to be alone.	Perhaps they were hurt when you pushed. They did not want to know about computers.	One punched you because you bothered them and hurt them.	You punched back much harder. Your reaction was over the top.

- Give drama lessons in your class and encourage the school to start up a drama class at lunch-times or after hours. Drama and acting can help teach how to act and react in specific situations. It promotes the use of appropriate facial expressions and tones of voice in various circumstances. It can also be used to role-play how to behave or react in difficult situations, such as when being bullied or when approached inappropriately. Often children with Asperger's are exceptionally good at acting as they love to have defined roles and know what is expected of them.

- As a teacher, use your body language in a careful way. Avoid arm-waving as you talk, as the child may think the movements mean something and will spend wasted time trying to work out what you want. If you need to point to the left, turn your body so that your left is the same as the child's left.

- Be aware that the child will not pick up your moods by your body stance. If you are trying to show anger or impatience by crossing your arms and frowning, then forget it. If you want the child to know you are angry about a specific incident, then say 'I am angry because of X.'

- Do not judge the child's moods by her stance. Crossed arms and a frown is no indication the child is unhappy. Most likely she just feels comfortable standing that way. An emotionless face is no indicator of the feelings underneath. 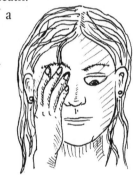 The child may be on the verge of a meltdown, or may feel quite happy, thank you very much. Words are a much greater indicator of feelings. If you are unsure if the child is angry, ask 'Are you angry?' Even then, be wary of the answer as the child may not be able to articulate how she feels and shrug off the difficult question with 'Dunno.'

- Do not insist that the child looks you in the eye when you talk. Often she finds this physically nauseating and invasive, as if her 'soul is being sucked out'. However, it is important that you work out some sort of signal that the child is listening to you. The child could perhaps look at your mouth or nose or eyebrows or learn to nod occasionally to show she is taking in what you say.

- The child with Asperger's will often gravitate to a teacher on duty in the playground as she feels safe in adult company. Use this time to discuss the body language of other children in the playground. Point out a smiling child and say 'See that girl laughing with her friends. How do you think she is feeling?'

Point out a child with a very sad face and say 'Look at the boy on the ground. His knee is bleeding. Do you think he is sad or hurt or angry?'

- For younger children, actively teach common body language signs. Finger to lips means quiet. Thumbs up means good work. Nodding means yes. Shaking head means no, and so on. Be aware that, in some cultures, the body language is different. In India, for example, people shake their heads for yes and nod for no, and looking directly into the eyes of someone in authority is considered very bad manners.

- Insist on good old-fashioned manners in your class. These basic interactions with others can give a child a script on how to behave initially in a situation. Adapt the formality of each situation appropriately. For example, it might be good manners to say to the headmaster 'Good morning, sir'; however, it is also good manners to say 'hey' to your mate. Manners to consider include:

  ◦ Greet others with 'Good morning. How are you today?' or appropriate variation.

  ◦ Answer greetings with 'I am well, thank you' or appropriate variation.

  ◦ Shake hands with guests.

  ◦ Say please and thank you.

  ◦ Open doors for others.

  ◦ Adults go first.

  ◦ Push your chair in when you leave the table. (See **Manners** in **Preparing for Your Student with Asperger Syndrome**.)

Classroom activities

- Start a body language scrap-book and collate pictures of happy/sad/angry/frustrated faces and situations, for example. Likewise, collate images where body language shows emotions – people holding hands, an angry person with arms crossed or fists clenched. Explore the extremes of how an emotion can be depicted. For example, anger can be someone screaming with their mouth open, or the narrowing of lips and squinting eyes. Make flash cards with the pictures of faces/bodies on one side and the emotion they are showing on the other. Encourage the child to get a body language app on her phone. Get the class to write a paragraph on what the person on the card might say next, or write what they might be thinking based on the expression alone.

- Put the children into groups and give out cards with a single word, or small sentence; for example, stop, wait, come here, go away, no way, great. Then each child in the group has to say the word with a different tone of voice and body stance to show very different meanings.

- Have an emotions day. Children write up all the emotions they see on each other's faces during the day. Make a game of it.

- Make up two sets of cards. One set contains everyday actions: drive a car; play tennis; walk the dog. The other set contains emotions: happy, sad, confused, and so on. The child has to select one card from each set and then act out the scenario; for example, walking the dog angrily.

- Select a child to come to the front of the class to wear a mask so that most facial features are covered. Select an emotion card from the previous activity. Without using words or sounds the child has to depict the emotion.

- Watch a scene from a movie with the sound off. Try and choose a scene where the emotions and 'feel' come through the words and music. Let the children guess what is happening. Then turn the sound back on. What they thought could have been a happy scene might have had scary music and a scream in the background. Or a scary scene might have been someone about to cry out in happiness. Explain how hard it would be if they had to guess all the time if things around them were scary or not scary. Let them imagine the troubles that could lead to. (See **Understanding the Perspectives of Others: Theory of Mind.**)

Home link

- Explain to parents the steps you are taking in class to assist the child in understanding body language and facial expressions. Encourage them to do the same, as the child will benefit greatly if all the activities you are doing are repeated at home.

- Encourage the parents to enrol the child into drama or acting lessons to assist in role-playing and learning rote responses to everyday happenings.

Literal Thinkers and Speakers

Description

People with Asperger Syndrome do not intuitively understand colloquialisms, sarcasm or turns of phrase. However, they can be taught. They may also speak in a monotone and be very frank in what they say without meaning disrespect or unkindness. If a child in your classroom appears to be cheeky or rude or does something out of character, sit back a moment and ask yourself what prompted the child's behaviour. It may be something you or someone else said that has been misinterpreted or your instructions or requests were ambiguous.

The child:

- does not pick up on hints; for example, if someone said, 'It would be great if the garbage was taken out', the child would most likely not realize he was actually being asked to do it

- does not translate a statement into a request for action; for example, 'Your food is getting cold' is not understood as 'Eat your food before it gets cold'

- does not understand idioms or metaphorical language; for example, sayings like 'Hop to it' or 'in a second' will be taken literally; 'Keep your hands to yourself' or 'Has the cat got your tongue' are downright confusing; and 'Wash your hands in the toilet' is outright disturbing

- does not always understand the humour or jokes of others and can have a sense of humour that others do not understand

- may use language in an unusual way as if he was a foreigner learning a new language

- may speak in a monotone or can have a strange rhythm to the sound of his voice

- can use long and complicated words and may sound very formal

- may correct others' grammatical errors or ways of speech

- may not understand the implications of emphasis on different words by others; for example, a person can say 'Great' when he is happy, sad or angry, but the child with Asperger's will understand the word as its dictionary meaning of a good thing

- may obey instructions very literally; for example, when asked to get his pencils, will only get pencils and not pens or the pencil case; when asked to put away his shoes will put away shoes, but not boots or sandals

- may get 'stuck' on a topic or issue and continually want clarification or a full understanding of what other people see as unimportant trivia; for example, to be 'good' at maths should you get 95% or 96% on a test? If you get 92% does that mean you are no longer good at maths? What about 95.4%? What if you get 100% one day, but 80% the next?

- may insist on following directions exactly and get upset or frustrated if this is not possible; for example, if a recipe asks for 2 cups of flour but only 5 or 6 cups are available, then is unable to continue cooking

- does not understand the hidden meanings behind words; for example, 'Let's go for a pizza' is often a gesture of friendship, but if the child does not like pizza he will not accept the offer; or might get to the pizza place and prefer a salad, but feels he has to buy a pizza

- does not understand exaggerations; for example, would not realize that 'I could eat a hundred burgers' simply means 'I am very hungry'

- will be very honest without thinking of the hidden agenda behind the words; for example, if asked 'Do I look fat in this?' or 'Do you think I am an idiot?' or 'Are you trying to be smart?' the child is likely to answer 'Yes'

- will say exactly what he thinks but is not trying to be rude or offensive; for example, 'Your breath smells like dead fish', 'You have a long nose', 'I don't like this present'

- may get disturbed by fictional stories; for example, thinks that a wolf is truly eating Red Riding Hood's grandmother

- can find homophones utterly confusing and can spend a lot of time being caught on a visual image trying to make sense of what was heard; for example, a king who reigns (rains); going around in bare (bear) feet; I read (red) a book; visit my aunt (ant)

- may be very literal about obeying rules; for example, may get distressed if he sees a sign in a library that says 'No eating or drinking' and does not realize the instructions are just for the library; may not be willing to enter an out-of-bounds area even if in attendance with a teacher

- may get very upset if others disobey rules, and can become a class policeman and try to enforce the rules on others

- may find it hard to follow verbal instructions

- may hate 'small' talk or social gatherings where casual talking is required

- may associate himself literally with songs and poems that mention 'I'; for example, may vigorously deny that he is a teapot in the nursery rhyme 'I'm a little teapot, short and stout' and will refuse to be 'tipped over and poured out'

- finds it hard to pick up on verbal clues in a conversation, such as when to stop talking and let the other person speak

- may find it hard to modulate the loudness of his voice

- may not moderate language for age or rank or situation; for example, may speak to a visiting dignitary in the same way he talks to his sister at home

- often prefers factual labels for people, rather than using names or nicknames; for example, will call parents 'my mother and my father', and call siblings 'boy and girl' rather than their names. A teacher is just that – 'teacher'

- may repeat what is said in a private moment, oblivious to the embarrassment it may cause; for example, 'Mr Lyall, Mum says your name is Mr Lie-a-lot'

- may not understand that a rule for one situation is applicable in another similar situation; for example, may get into trouble for calling Tom an idiot so promises not to do so again, then calls Bill an idiot; or promises not to eat biscuits without permission, but then eats cake without permission

- may hate talking on the phone

- may answer questions literally without answering or obeying the larger implied question or implication; for example, will

answer 'Yes' to 'Can you get me a glass of water?' but not get the water

- May answer poorly worded test questions literally and fail the test; for example, 'Do you think that…' may prompt a single-word answer, 'Yes' or 'No.'

HOW YOUR STUDENT MAY EXPLAIN IT

- ☼ Why can't people just say what they mean? I can understand words perfectly well. I am not stupid. But if you try to hint things to me, or use a tone of voice that I have to magically understand, or I have to decipher stupid sentences that don't make any sense at all, then I won't understand you. And it is always me who is to blame and has to change. I simply do not understand why people think that is fair.

- ☼ I really, really try to behave. I try to obey. I try to understand what you say. And then when I do exactly what is asked of me, I get into trouble.

- ☼ I don't like lies and I don't like lying. It disturbs me a lot to think that contradictory things could be believed because of something I said, so I always say the truth. I cannot bear the thought that I will believe something wrong because I trusted the person who said it. It's not that I am trying to do the right thing all the time. It's just that I hate to be confused and I hate to confuse others. The order of truth must be kept.

- ☼ When I saw my grandfather and asked him to drink like a fish, just like Mother said he did, I got into trouble. Then I found out that it is okay for Mother to say things about Grandfather when he can't hear her, but I can't say the same things when he can hear. How am I supposed to understand that?

At school

- Speak as clearly and as correctly as possible and use complete sentences. For example, if showing a picture of a car, say 'This is a picture of car' and not 'This is a car.' Say 'Put the book on my table' and not 'Put that over there.'

- Be specific with instructions. Say 'Do not lean back on the legs of your chair' and not 'Stop that!'

- Slow down your speech, but do not dumb down your language. Your student is not stupid, but needs extra time to process what you say.

- Be specific with praise. Say 'Your clay pot is made very well' and not 'That looks great.'

- Be specific when chastising. Say 'It was wrong to punch Jane in the arm' and not 'That was very naughty.'

- Do not use sarcasm. To say 'Well, that was clever' when a child spills the paint will confuse him no end, and may result in the paint being spilt every session.

- Understand that your student may find it very hard to follow verbal instructions for many reasons. Maybe you used abbreviations or colloquialisms he does not understand. Perhaps you speak too fast. Maybe the child got caught on a word or saying that did not make sense and was unable to listen to the rest of your instructions. Perhaps the noise level in the class was too high for your student to hear clearly. Perhaps he was distracted by other sensory input. Don't forget that the child with Asperger's is a visual learner. For all these reasons, write instructions on a board, or a hand-out sheet. If a child only has to do 'up to number 10', then mark number 10 with a red marker so it is clear when to stop.

- Keep to your word. If you say that the child can have five minutes on the computer as a reward, the child will expect five minutes and not 4½ minutes. If you say 'We will do that tomorrow', then the child will expect that you will do that tomorrow. If you have to break you word, then explain the reasons clearly to the child and not expect him to just 'go with the flow'.

- If the child needs medical attention, then explain each step so the child is not surprised by sudden pain or touch: 'I am going to wash the cut to clean out the dirt. This may hurt just a little bit, but it is important to get rid of any germs that may infect the cut. Then I will put on ointment and a bandage to keep the cut clean and help it to heal.'

- Try not to be offended if your student seems rude, but is in fact just being honest. If he tells you that your hair looks like a bird's nest then explain that it is inappropriate to say personal things about a teacher. Remind him not to say anything that might make another person feel bad. In your class, make a policy that if you can't say something that is kind or polite, then don't make personal comments at all. The child may well come back and say 'But if my hair looked like a bird's nest, I wouldn't care if you told me. I like birds and their nests are clever.' Okay, well, this is never going to be easy. But persevere and over time guide the child to inoffensive speech through repetition and gentle correction.

- Try not to be offended if the child corrects your mistakes and those of his peers. He is not trying to be belligerent or arrogant or a know-it-all but rather is genuinely trying to be helpful. Often the child feels a physical reaction to the 'discord' of incorrect information. The world is not right when untruths are out there. If necessary, take the child aside and explain how people feel when mistakes are pointed out publicly. Help the child to assess the situation as to when to make a correction. It would not be good to point out to a bully that the correct grammar is 'What are you doing here?' and not 'Wotcha doin?' However, there are times when even a teacher may need blatant errors corrected, such as getting the capital city of a country wrong.

- If your young student gets very distressed during story time then consider what you are reading. If a big giant is picking up children and threatening death, the child may think this could truly happen to him.

- If your student seems to be deliberately disobedient or disrespectful, take a moment to reflect on what you or others said, or how a question was phrased. It is highly possible that the child took a literal interpretation of what was said and reacted accordingly.

- Be aware of how other students in the classroom may manipulate or abuse the child's naïvety and literal thinking and speaking. They may encourage silly questions, or make fun of the child's 'robot'-like voice. They may dare him to do something and so he feels obliged to go ahead and do it. Often this ends in the child getting into trouble and taking the blame all by himself. Or the child may eventually react physically or verbally and again get into trouble. Always be very wary when your Asperger student harms another child or blatantly disobeys rules. The chances are that another child is directly involved. Be sure that punishments are fair, predictable, and that the students who encouraged or taunted the child with Asperger's are also punished. (See **Bullying**.)

- Be aware that it is very difficult for a child with Asperger's to modulate the loudness of his voice. To help the child to speak with the right amount of volume, observe people in different situations and rate the loudness of a voice from 1 to 5 with 1 being a whisper and 5 being a shout. Then when going into a library, for instance, say 'Use your number 1 voice', or when giving an answer in class, 'Use your number 4 voice.'

- The child may not know when to join a conversation or when to stop talking and does not pick up on subtle hints. Give clear instructions about not interrupting when the teacher is talking, such as 'Raise your hand if you want to speak.' Teach the child ways to enter a conversation, such as saying 'Can I tell you something?' (See **Forming Friendships and Following Social Rules**.)

Classroom activities

- Give out cards to various children with a scenario on them; they have to act that scenario and include the words 'Come here.' Examples could be a monster wanting to eat up little children, a mother wanting to give someone an ice-cream, a headteacher wanting to give an award, a bully wanting to punch someone. Explain how we know which actor is pretending to be a good person, and who is pretending to be someone who could harm you. Look at their faces and hand gestures and body language. Explain how hard it would be if you could only hear the words and nothing else.

- Make up a class book on idioms and sayings and their meanings, and then have the children illustrate it. Investigate idioms from different countries.

- Speak to the class in a very angry tone, but say kind words; for example, 'You are lovely sweet kids, and I am glad that I am your teacher' but say it with a frown and arms folded. Then say something unkind in a nice way; for example, smile as you say 'You are terrible kids and I wish I wasn't your teacher.' Discuss how this is very confusing, as your body says one thing, but your voice says another. Show how your tone of voice and your body language together make up how people understand you. (See **Body Language Blindness**.)

- Talk to the class in a language they don't understand, or make up a pretend language. Point to one child and gesture for him to leave the classroom. Speak in your pretend language and make your tone of voice insistent until the child obeys and starts to leave the room. Then switch back to your normal language and explain that you wanted him to open a window. Discuss how the confusion took place. Your language was not understood and your non-verbal language was confusing. Discuss whose fault it was that the child 'disobeyed' the teacher in trying to leave the room when he was supposed to open a window. Discuss how if there is a breakdown in verbal and non-verbal communication then people might get into trouble through no fault of their own, and that others may get frustrated and angry if they are misunderstood. (See **Body Language Blindness**.)

Home link

- Go through the list of literal thinking and speaking traits and help the parents and carers to see how and why their child may act and react in certain ways.

- Explain that the child may have problems talking on the phone due to a number of reasons, for example: the inability to watch the speaker's mouth for extra clues as to what is being said; difficulties in focusing on the one sound coming through the phone and having to drown out all other sounds heard; fear that his own voice will be too loud or too soft, or be misunderstood and may have to repeat himself. Help the child overcome this by having mock telephone conversations. Make sure the child, at the very least, knows how to call emergency services.

Forming Friendships and Following Social Rules

Description

Forming friendships and following social rules is one of the hardest things for a child with Asperger Syndrome to do. In fact, in many ways, this is what defines a person with Asperger's. She is often the loner, the one who finds it hard to make friends, the socially awkward one who  makes social gaffes, and talks about her interests all the time. She is ostracized because of the tone of voice or the way she walks or her lack of interest in things peers consider important.

If a man walks around with a white stick and dark glasses it is easy to tell that he is blind and those around him would rush to help him if he stumbled or fell. The social 'blindness' of those with Asperger's gives no visible clues for those around them to know about this disability. Consequently when they 'stumble' they are regarded as insensitive or arrogant or boorish or lots of other words that aren't nice. Unfortunately, wearing a big sign that says 'I am socially blind' is not an option so there are only two ways for this to be dealt with. One: those who know of this blindness, such as parents and teachers and carers and siblings, give all the support and guidance they can. And two: the person with Asperger's needs to learn the hard edges and pointy bits of society in order to avoid them.

Although a blind person can never be taught to see, a person with Asperger's can be taught social norms and rules and can adapt and fit in quite comfortably to most social situations even if her understanding of the taught social norms are functional rather than intrinsic. It is a bit like teaching a colour-blind person that the top traffic light is red. She will always then stop when the top light is lit, rather than at the 'red' light, but the effect is the same: she stops at the right time.

Social blindness affects many other aspects of the child's life and is intricately linked to many other aspects of Asperger Syndrome.

The child:

- finds it hard to pick up on unspoken rules and hidden agendas in social settings and may rely on learned behaviour to fit in

- does not know how to initiate social conversations

- finds it hard to make friends and may be bullied

- may say that she feels like an alien dropped into a strange land where nothing makes sense

- finds other people's behaviours illogical and confusing

- does not pick up other people's body language

- does not like to look others in the eyes

- may bore others by going on about a favourite topic or special interest

- is not usually influenced by peer pressure to conform

- finds it hard to engage in social banter and to continue small talk

- finds it hard to tell if she is being teased or encouraged and does not understand if someone is being nice or mean to her

- may find it hard to play pretend games and prefer logical games such as chess or computer games; does not know how to take turns in a game; does not understand the rules of team sports, especially the unwritten ones; is often chosen last in sporting teams and groups

- may change the topic in a conversation without others understanding why she has gone in that direction

- may presume that others know what she is thinking and therefore begin a conversation in mid-story

- may ramble in a conversation, without reaching a coherent point, as she may be speaking for her own benefit and not to particularly inform others

- may say inappropriate things in a conversation as she does not realize what is acceptable in that situation

- does not pick up on non-verbal gestures

- does not pick up on meanings behind inflections and tones of voice

- does not understand sarcasm

- takes things very literally

- needs time away from people to unwind, especially after a social outing

- finds social interactions exhausting and may avoid large groups, parties, and so on

- does not comprehend why her peers enjoy noisy, social gatherings

- does not usually like to be hugged or touched, especially by those not close to her

- often finds things like make-up and fashion (for girls) and football and sports (for boys) uninteresting

- does not intuitively understand social boundaries and may stand too close to another person

- may follow people around, talking to them as they move

- prefers to have just one or two friends and does not seek to be in a large group

- prefers to work alone rather than in groups

- finds it hard to understand the emotional and physical needs of others

- appears to lack empathy

- may be physically awkward in a social setting, not knowing how to stand, how to sit naturally, where to put hands, where to look, and so on

- may find the sensory issues in a social situation overwhelming; for example, loud noises, smells of food and people, crowds that bump and push.

SEE ALSO

Adapting to Change

Understanding the Perspectives of Others: Theory Of Mind

Literal Thinkers and Speakers

Apparent Lack of Emotions

Meltdowns

Special Interests

Bullying

HOW YOUR STUDENT MAY EXPLAIN IT

☿ All my life people have judged me before they knew me. It's like I had a sign on my head saying 'I'm different and weird. Stay away!' And then I am told it is my fault that no one wants to be my friend. How do they know they don't want to be my friend if they don't know me?

☿ I feel that I live inside the game 'Whack a Mole'. Every time I raise my head in a social situation, I get bopped by someone who tells me to shut up, to get lost, to mind my own business. I am called names, pushed over, my things are stolen and destroyed. I am not invited to parties and no one plays with me. And why does this happen? You know, I have no idea. I went to a party once. I was forced to sit with a cousin I didn't know and I knew I wouldn't meet again in a long time. I had no idea what to say. My stomach clenched and I breathed fast as I thought of the myriad things I had learned about small talk. I could talk about the weather. (It was hot. That bit was over in a second.) I could ask where he had come from but I didn't want to know. I could compliment him on something, but there was nothing about him I particularly liked. I knew I couldn't mention that his breath smelt like garlic or that he had a stain on his shirt. The music was loud. I couldn't think, so I said nothing and got up and went outside. I played with the dog until Mum found me hours later. The dog was nice, so the party wasn't a complete waste of time.

    Do you know what it is like to be chosen last? The sick wells up inside you as you know you are not wanted. Again. Other kids sneer and screw up their faces when you are finally forced upon their team. I don't know faces well, but I know those faces. Sometimes I am kicked by my own side just because I exist. They think I don't care or that I don't hear or feel anything. They call me Robot. But inside, I am twisting and churning and puking.

At school

The importance of your students having friends cannot be underestimated. Friends help each other to understand things around them. They support and protect each other. They help bring humour to a situation. When a child has no friends, so many things start to go wrong in her life. The isolated child is at risk of bullying. She cannot turn to another for clarification or help. She cannot share things that interest and excite her.

One of the best ways you can promote your Asperger student as 'good friend potential' is to build up her self-esteem and promote her strong points. Over and over again parents report that a huge impact on their child's social life is due directly to the teacher's attitude to that child. If the teacher belittles, the class belittles. If the teacher thinks the child is clever and worthwhile, the class follows suit. Spend time with your Asperger student. Listen to her. Promote an atmosphere of trust so the child is relaxed about coming to you for assistance and support. If chastisement is needed, then do it fairly, and preferably privately, without embarrassing your student in front of others. In other words, treat your students with respect and this will spill over into their attitudes towards one another.

It is also important to understand that the child with Asperger's finds it very difficult to follow social norms and to make friends. There are many ways in which you can help with these difficulties in your classroom. Here are some:

- Give the child as many opportunities to socialize as possible, while recognizing that sometimes the child needs alone or quiet time to rest, to recharge and to simply be away from people. Put the child into group-work and then support the group. Put the child into sporting teams but be there to guide and demystify the rules. Have class parties and help the child mix. Build up the child's self-esteem by showing that she is a valuable member of the class. Allow the child to mentor another in her special interest. Let the child be a buddy to a younger child. Give the child responsibilities and praise when these are achieved. Put on class plays and give the child a role she enjoys. Make the child a valued and special member of your class.

- If you notice that your student is butting into conversations or dominating a discussion, then gently remind her to take turns to talk. Take the time to explain the social expectations involved. Help the child understand that other people want to have their say too. Make sure that you do give the child a chance to speak and share her thoughts.

- Explain to the child that if she wants to join in a conversation socially with other people, rather than coming up to a group and immediately launching into a monologue about her favourite thing, rather sit back a moment and see what the group is talking about. Don't stare at the people, but rather glance at them occasionally. If the child knows a little about what the group is talking about, then wait for a pause in the conversation then move a little closer and the people will most likely look up and notice her. When they make eye contact, then the child can contribute something on the topic, either by making a comment or giving an opinion or asking a question. The child knows that she is accepted in the conversation if the people start talking on the topic with the child, and they look at her, with their bodies facing her. If the people do not want the child to enter the conversation, they will turn away or not talk to the child on the topic. Let the child know that sometimes people will want her to join and sometimes they won't. If the child is not wanted, rather than standing there and annoying the group, then she should casually walk away.

- In fact, in all situations where you see your Asperger student breaking social rules, talk to her about it. Do not yell at the child or get upset. Explain what 'rule' she was breaking and help her work out a way to not repeat the incident. Try not to dismiss a social rule by saying 'That's just how it is', or 'It's just not polite', as this is not helpful at all to the child trying to understand. If possible, explain the rule. Unfortunately, some rules just can't be explained. After all, what really is the harm in asking a lady how old she is?

- Seat the child at the end of rows where she is not crowded by others. Be sure that the person she is sitting next to is not aggressive towards the child in any way.

- Discover the child's interests (which are usually easy to know as she will talk about them all the time) and direct her to other like-minded children. Allow the child to present the special interest to the class, or if it is school-related, let her be the teacher for a lesson.

- Start up a club in the lunch-time or after hours for students with similar interests.

- Take the time to meet the parents of your students. A sympathetic parent may be very willing to invite a lonely child to a birthday party or have the child over for a play-date with their own child. Parental support goes a long way towards children becoming friends.

- Always listen to both sides of the story in times of conflict. This helps both the student with Asperger's and the ones without to understand that they each had reasons for what they did.

- Arrange a buddy system in your school where an older child is assigned to help out with a younger child. Choose the older child very carefully for your child with Asperger's. Match interests if possible. Alternatively, make the child with Asperger's a buddy to a younger child.

- Be aware of the dangers of lunch-time and free time where the children are left to their own devices without teacher input. This is a time when your child may be bullied or ostracized. Give safe alternatives to being alone, such as going to the library or a computer room, or have some supervised activity such as a club or special interest meeting.

- If you put your students into groups for class work or sporting teams, choose the children for each group carefully and match the child with Asperger's with those in the class who relate to her best. The child with Asperger's often prefers to work alone rather than in groups, so if possible allow this option.

Warn the child ahead of time that groups will be coming up as this is one of those surprises children with Asperger's do not like. Help the group split up the tasks evenly so all children know exactly what they have to do.

• Help the child understand that some topics are not suitable for children to talk about in the classroom and that there are things that are best not to mention out of the classroom either. If the child strays into inappropriate talk, often all she needs is a prompting to stop. If necessary, take the child aside and explain what is, and what is not, appropriate talk in different situations. For example, it is okay to ask another child how old he is, but not an adult. Don't talk about things that are sexual in nature, or mention personal body parts, in the classroom or to people who are not close trusted friends or family members. Don't say things about how people look or smell unless they are compliments.

• Don't forget that your student is a visual learner. When the child breaks a social rule, write up a cartoon strip showing what happened and what rule was broken and how a similar incident can be avoided in the future.

• Do not let the child use her Asperger's as an excuse for not having friends or behaving in an unacceptable way. Instead, motivate the child to improve her social skills and teach her ways to fit in. Things like dressing like others do, looking after personal hygiene, having good manners, listening to others, learning social etiquettes of greetings and responses all go a very long way towards the child being accepted by peers.

• Remember how hard your student has to work at coping daily in the classroom. Give her time out to rest and recuperate. Send the child on errands to let her get away from the class for a while. Provide a quiet, safe corner where she can retreat to when things get too overwhelming.

Classroom activities

- Divide your class into groups. Give a scenario where ten people are on a sinking boat: an old doctor, a five-year-old girl, a baby boy and his mother, the captain of the ship, a man with only one leg, a maid, a wealthy businessman, a fisherman and a teenager who has dropped out of school. Or make up your own characters. Explain that there are only places for eight on the lifeboat. Have the children discuss who should be left behind. Talk about how each person brings their own strengths and weaknesses to any situation and how each person could bring some benefit to others. Even the baby and little girl could bring hope that young life survives a disaster and gives the others someone to nurture and protect. Relate this to the classroom where each student has a strength to contribute.

- If your student with Asperger's gets too close to other students, or follows them around as she talks, or alternatively if other children invade your student's personal space, then try this activity. Show a series of images where a lot of people are in close proximity to each other (e.g. on a bus, in a packed train, in a sporting crowd, in a busy queue). Focus on people's faces. They might look bored or frustrated or tired but are rarely scared or uncomfortable. Now look at images where just a few people are close to each other but are happy (e.g. girls giggling in a group, friends walking hand-in-hand, boys giving high fives or rough hugs at a sports game). Talk about when it is good and acceptable to be in another person's personal space. Now show examples where close proximity is uncomfortable (e.g. someone not liking a hug, someone sitting too close to another on a relatively empty train or bus). Have two students come to the front and walk towards each other right up until they are almost touching noses. Discuss with them when they started to feel uncomfortable about being so close to the other person. Discuss the importance of not invading another person's personal space and give verbal cues on how to let others know you are uncomfortable; for example, 'You are in my personal space', 'Please don't sit so close', 'I don't like it when you follow me around like that.'

- For the younger children, make up a 'Good and Bad Words' chart. Next to a smiley face write words that make others feel good: Come and play with me; You are my friend; I like you; You are clever; You make me happy. Beside a crying face write words that make others feel bad: Go away; I don't like you; You are not my friend; Shut up; You are stupid. Promote the use of accepting words in your classroom.

Home link

- Encourage the carers to give the child as many opportunities as possible to socialize with others. If the child is reluctant and would prefer to spend time on a special interest, rather than giving in and not forcing the child to mix, be supportive and give her assistance and guidance on how to mix. Have the child join a sporting team to help provide a friendship base, being aware she is more likely to enjoy one with limited team work, for example running or fencing rather than football or cricket. Speech and drama and acting lessons are excellent for reinforcing social behaviours as often the script helps the child speak and act in a socially acceptable way, at least while on stage.

- Encourage carers to invite other children home on play-dates and, if necessary, suggest children from your class who already get on well with the child.

- Encourage the carers to foster an environment in the home where the child is valued for her special interest gifts, and to give opportunities for the child to share the interest with others, especially with the view of promoting new friendships.

Join clubs with like-minded people. Perhaps the child could become a tutor or mentor for another student with the same interest.

- Explain the importance of giving the child opportunities to speak about social issues, especially if the child is depressed or anxious or expresses sadness at not fitting in and not having friends. It may be necessary for the child to have social skills classes or talk to a counsellor.

Apparent Lack of Emotions

Description

People with Asperger's can find it difficult to identify and describe emotions or empathy, and can be accused of having no emotions at all as they may not react in a way others expect; for example, they may not outwardly show sadness at news of a death. This condition of not showing signs of expected emotions has its own name – *alexithymia*. It can also be linked with body language blindness when the correct emotion for a situation may not be shown simply because the person with Asperger's has not picked up the signals that a response is required. However, those with Asperger's express strongly that they do indeed feel emotions, often even stronger than the 'average' person, but show those emotions in a different way than expected by others. They may not read the signals, but they do care.

The child:

- may have a limited vocabulary to describe his own emotions, though this does not mean that no emotions are present, just that the child does not have the words to describe them; for example, the child may feel great sadness at hearing of a friend's cat dying, but simply not know what is the right thing to say so may walk away without a response, which causes others to think he does not care

- may have delayed empathy or emotion; for example, may hear of the death of someone close and not immediately feel anything but later thinks about it and feels overwhelming sadness

- may confuse emotions; for example, smile when feeling scared, frown when feeling happy or laugh or cry at inappropriate times

- may express many emotions with one emotion; for example, may show unhappiness, confusion, fear and anger all as anger

- can find it very difficult to read the emotions of others

- may restrain his negative emotions for a long time (like the time spent at school) and then suddenly explode in a fit of anger or have a meltdown at a seemingly minor incident

- may presume that another person's emotions are directly related to him; for example, if the teacher is angry, may automatically feel it is his fault when it may have nothing to do with the child

- may flap or jump to show extreme emotions such as happiness or fear

- may rationalize, rather than 'feel', emotions

- may only truly feel another's emotions once he has experienced that same emotion

- may remain calm at times when other people panic

- may express love or sympathy by doing something nice for the person, or being well behaved, rather than giving a hug or words of comfort

- may not read body language or understand nuances of people's voices, so if someone who is upset says 'I am fine' then the child may accept that at face value and then be accused of being uncaring or unemotional

- may find it easier to express emotions through writing, art, music or poetry

- may learn about emotions from reading fiction written in the first person.

SEE ALSO

Adapting to Change

Body Language Blindness

HOW YOUR STUDENT MAY EXPLAIN IT

- When I was little and I felt things strongly, I used to ask my mum what face I had to use. She would tell me things like smile if someone did something nice for me or frown if I was worried about someone. Even now I remember her lessons and can hear her voice and use the right face even if I still don't really understand why I am using it.

- It's like I am on one side of frosted glass. I try very hard to let other people know how I feel. However, all my little movements and gestures are not seen at all, and people think I don't feel anything. So I scream and jump up and down, and they can see this, but don't know why I am doing it or what it means. I am living in a frosty glass cage. Sometimes I want to break out. Other times I give up trying to communicate as it is too much effort.

- When I say that I don't know what is wrong, I mean it. I am not trying to push you away. I am not just keeping things to myself. I genuinely don't know what is wrong. It might take me hours or even days to understand what has upset me. Or I may never know. Don't ask me over and over, 'What's wrong?' Give me space.

- Oh, I have emotions alright. When you reject me, and degrade me, and mock me, I feel those things. I feel them so deeply and for so long that they never go away. Years and years later I still feel them. I am only a robot on the outside. Inside, I hurt like any human. Maybe more so.

At school

The best thing you can do in a classroom situation is to be aware that a child with Asperger's *does* have emotions. His face may not show the depth of the feelings that are going on inside his mind but that does not mean that no feelings are being felt. Some children have expressed an extreme empathy with others that can be so crippling that their bodies do not react as others react. Others can use logical steps to understand a situation to its conclusion and their expressed emotions may be the conclusion, not the feelings originally felt.

For example, Bob sees a friend, Jack, cut his foot badly on some broken glass in the classroom. Here are four different scenarios of how Bob may show his emotions:

Bob knows the cut would hurt and is worried if Jack is okay. →	The cut was caused by glass that has now been picked up. →	Bob knows that same glass can't cut him so he is glad. →	Bob smiles. Others think Bob is happy that Jack is hurt.
Bob knows the cut would hurt and is worried if Jack is okay. →	The teacher is looking after Jack very well. →	Bob knows there is nothing more he can do to help. →	Bob goes back to work. Others think he doesn't care.
Bob knows the cut would hurt and is worried if Jack is okay. →	Bob says to Jack 'Are you okay?' →	Jack says 'I'm just great.' →	Bob believes him and goes back to work. Others think he doesn't care.
Bob knows the cut would hurt and wonders how he can help Jack. →	While he stands there, others help Jack. →	Others think 'Bob just stood there and did nothing.' →	Later Bob is very sad that Jack was hurt. He buys Jack a battery charger as a gift.

If you, as a teacher, can begin to understand some of these situations then you will realize how complex the world of emotions is to someone with Asperger's. And understanding is a great thing.

Here are some ways you can help:

- When you see your student displaying socially unacceptable emotions, for example giggling when someone is hurt, or seemingly showing no emotions at all, then talk to the child alone. Do not question him in front of his peers. Try to understand what he was thinking. Explain which emotions are appropriate to use in a specific situation.

- Give correct names to emotions; for example, a child may be expressing fear but calling it anger.

- Gives names to your own emotions and state why you feel that way. If angry, do not say 'You naughty child. Get out of my sight!' Say 'I am very angry because you ripped John's book. I want you to go to your quiet corner for five minutes to let us both calm down and then we can talk.'

- Often people with Asperger's find it easier to write down their emotions and explain their actions in print than to verbalize them. If the child is upset about something or is in trouble and he can't tell you why, encourage him to write about it.

- Do not use sarcasm to try to elicit a response of sorrow or shame over the child's actions. For example, imagine you intercept a note that your Asperger student wrote that says 'I hate this class. Mr B sounds like a buzz saw.' If you drawl sarcastically, 'Well, I am ssoooooo sorry that you don't like the sound of my voice. Would you like me to sound more like trickling water?' then your student may well be very honest and say 'Yes.' It would be much better to talk to your student about the note after the class. Or simply realize that the child is telling the truth from his perspective and is not trying to be disrespectful, so then you ignore the note.

- If your student suddenly erupts in a fit of anger, or goes into a meltdown at a seemingly insignificant trigger, then take the time to assess what may have gone on before this. Had the child tried to get your attention, but seemed calm and emotionless or spoke in a monotone voice, so you ignored his 'minor' complaint? Was something different in the classroom that may have caused the child to feel anxious or unsettled? Was there an overload on any one of the senses – extra noise, strong fumes in the class, fans on? All these things can cause an emotional response in the child that he is mostly likely not able to articulate or explain but, once this builds up, needs to be expressed in some way. Before any punishment is given, talk to the child (when he has calmed down) to see if you can together work out what went wrong. Then devise a plan to stop it happening again.

- For a younger child, or one with limited speech, make up visual cards so the child can point to how he feels. At first these might be very basic: happy, sad, angry. Gradually increase the range to include fear, frustration, sorry, and so on.

- Create a quiet corner where the child is allowed to go whenever he likes in order to calm down and control his emotions. Alternatively, if you see the child is restless and anxious, allow a toilet break, or send the child on an errand. Anything to give him space to collect himself.

Classroom activities

- Watch a movie with the sound off and discuss the emotions the actors are feeling, judging by their facial expressions and body language.

- Make up or buy a sheet of people's faces with different emotions. Help the child learn the correct facial features for different emotions, so that he can

recognize them in others and use the correct expression when he feels an emotion.

Home link

- Discuss with caregivers how a child with Asperger's has difficulty showing emotions in a way that is understood by others. Go through the description at the beginning of this chapter to help them understand their own child.

- Keep an open relationship with carers and discuss regularly things that help you in the classroom to understand the child's emotions and needs, and in turn how you try to help the child to understand other's emotions and needs. Ask them about things that help at home.

Meltdowns

Description

A meltdown is where a child completely loses control of her behaviours and may, for example, scream, thrash, throw herself on the floor, hit out, bite. Naturally this can be very distressing for all involved. A meltdown is not to be confused with a temper tantrum, where a child is using similar behaviours in order to get her way or manipulate a situation. A child having a tantrum will often check to see if anyone is watching; will make sure she doesn't get hurt; and can turn off the tears as soon as she gets what she wants.

Those with Asperger Syndrome do not have a meltdown on purpose. They are not using their behaviour to manipulate the situation or to get their own way and they do not check if others are watching. Although the trigger might seem to be that the child did not get something desired, the actual cause of the meltdown is the inability to express or control the build-up of emotions, such as frustration, regret, anger, sadness, fear; or a meltdown can be caused by an overload on one or more of the senses. Some people with Asperger's describe a meltdown as a red or grey band across their eyes accompanied by a complete loss of control. Others describe a feeling of being a powerless observer outside of their bodies. However they describe it, they do not enjoy meltdowns, and never have one on purpose. It is vital to remember that despite how difficult a meltdown is for the teacher and fellow students, it is much, much harder for the child having the meltdown. After the meltdown is over, the child should be treated with compassion even as the repercussions unfold.

During a meltdown, the child:

- screams, thrashes, lashes out, kicks, bites

- may feel a red or grey band across her eyes

- does not check or seem to care if others are watching

- may fight or hit the person (including parents, fellow students and teachers) who seemingly triggered the meltdown

- may harm herself and others unintentionally

- may have anger so severe and so short-lived that she may honestly have no recollection of the incident, making her appear to be lying if the hurt or damage caused is denied

- feels powerless and completely out of control and cannot stop the meltdown at will

- will not be placated by a solution to the trigger; for example, if the meltdown was seemingly caused because she couldn't watch a TV show, then allowing the child to watch the show will not stop the meltdown

- may feel very depressed after the incident.

HOW YOUR STUDENT MAY EXPLAIN IT

- I panic. Can't breathe. It's like I have no skin and nothing holds me in. Every input is agony – sight, sound, everything. It's not pain or fear, not really, but it's both of those things and everything is utterly, completely wrong. I have to get away. Have to. Have to. If I can't, then I hit out at anything. Everything. Others. Myself.

- My body trembles. My mind goes blank. Something presses on me, pressing down and down, like thick invisible walls. I can't breathe and tension builds up and up inside me. All my Asperger traits intensify a million-fold. I flap, can't look at people, line things up in order, say the same words over and over, 'He did it. Hedidit. Hedidithedidit.' Then I blank out and explode.

- After a meltdown, I hate knowing what I have done. I go into a blank world where I have no emotion left at all. Like a robot. Drained and too exhausted to make the effort to feel anything. I try to stay away from others and get into my interest area that helps me calm down. I can stay this way for days.

At school

Before a meltdown

Often meltdowns are preceded by warning signals, and if you can learn to spot these signals, and alleviate the situation, then a meltdown can be avoided. Be aware that triggers for a meltdown are not always obvious. Asperger children may not even know their own triggers and so do not know how to explain them to others. Sometimes they might complain about something but it is pushed aside by an adult as unimportant or whining, and is therefore ignored. The child may use a monotone voice when telling of a grievance, or her facial expressions may be neutral, giving the adult no real hint of the frustration going on inside.

Here are some ways you can help to avoid a meltdown:

- Where meltdowns happen at a place a child visits regularly, such as home, school, a sporting facility or friend's place, have a pre arranged time-out area where the child can go to, to calm down. Make it clear this is not a 'punishment corner' but rather a safe place to allow the child to regain control. This place could contain pillows or a bean bag or a place to lie down. It could also contain calm music, a repetitive activity, like colouring-in or building blocks, a mini-trampoline or stress-relieving toys. It should not contain sharp items that a child in full meltdown mode could hurt herself with or on.

- Explain to the child the body changes that happen with rising anger and frustration. Fists clench. Teeth clench. Tummy tightens. Muscles tighten. Breath comes faster. Explain how these are warning signals that the child is stressed and it is time to go to a calming or safe place. Teach anger management techniques. Breathe deeply. Count to ten. Take yourself away from the situation if possible. Bounce on a mini-trampoline.

Squeeze a stress ball. Hold a comfort item. Deep pressure therapy. Whatever works.

- Model behaviour management techniques yourself. If the child is annoying you or you feel at screaming point because of her behaviours, don't yell or lash out with hurtful remarks, but say calmly, 'Your behaviour is upsetting me very much. It is best if we both have a little time apart so we can both calm down. I would like you to go to your safe place and rest a little while.' Or alternatively, you leave the classroom in the care of an assistant and go and have a chamomile tea!

- Learn triggers. Help the child avoid situations where the stress is high. Warn them in advance of change of routine. Avoid places where sensory input is excessive. Allow the child access to a quiet place such as a pillow corner or the library when input becomes too much. Divert attention if possible.

- Teach the child to ask appropriate questions or say safe phrases if she is afraid or confused or feels a meltdown coming on: 'I am getting angry', 'Please stop that', 'Did you mean that or was it an accident?', 'Are you trying to hurt me?'

- Listen carefully to a child's complaints. If an adult ignores the frustration build-up, then a meltdown is more likely to occur.

- Be consistent. If a child is allowed to do or have something one day and is refused it the next then understandably she will become frustrated.

- Pick your battle. It may not be worth your energy and the child's frustration if you insist she cannot play with a favourite, but disgusting, well-loved toy. But stand your ground if, for example, she hurts other children, or runs away from the classroom.

- Reward good behaviour rather than constantly picking on bad behaviour. And use terms such as, 'You are very clever (or wise or smart)', rather than a generalized 'Well done.'

- Don't condemn for something not understood. If you see children becoming stressed by something you asked them to do, then go over things again more slowly so that they understand what is asked of them and why.

- Speak in a quiet, soothing way. Acknowledge the child's distress and offer a choice of solutions to the immediate problem. This way the child feels like she is being respected and has a degree of control over the situation.

- If the child starts to get upset, act like a GPS giving instructions. When you make the wrong turn in your car, the machine does not yell at you but calmly says 'Now turn left at the next intersection.' If you can calmly ignore what the child has done wrong and state clearly what is expected next, then the child is most likely to obey and calm down in the process.

- As a last resort, allow the child some time in a special interest to calm down. This must be used very carefully or you will rapidly programme the child to yell and get upset in order to get access to the special interest.

During a meltdown

- Clear the area of other people and remove things on which child could hurt herself.

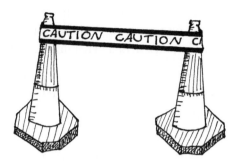

- The teacher, or parent or carer, must stay calm. Remember that no matter how hard the situation is for the adult, *it is much, much harder for the child.*

- Delegate only one person to deal with the child. If more than one person is trying to talk, then this confuses the child even more.

- Do not ask 'What's wrong?' or tell the child to 'Snap out of it' or demean the child in any way. At this stage, the child is incapable of listening to reason. In the child's mind, she is in fight/flight mode and is fighting for her life. Forget talking and bribery and common sense, and simply stand back.

- Eliminate as many senses as possible: dim lights, turn off loud sounds or close windows if the sounds are outside, send away people who are talking or yelling, turn off the TV, remove items with strong smells, including anyone wearing strong scents, and so on.

- *Never* grab or constrain a child unless she is a danger to herself or others. It is much, much better to simply watch over a child in meltdown than to barge in and try to stop it.

- Protect the child from unwarranted attention as much as possible. Do not let a crowd form around the child to watch and laugh.

- Never allow the situation to be filmed or photographed, especially if this is later used against her in social media. However, if a film is made for the express purpose of allowing the child to watch and learn from the situation, this may be of some benefit.

After a meltdown

- Keep in mind that the child has just gone through a very traumatic experience and may be feeling devastated when confronted with the harm or damage she may have caused. Be as calm and as gentle as you can. Try to push aside your own feelings of anger and frustration. If you are feeling upset, it may be best to allow another responsible adult, such as a school counsellor, to deal with the situation and help the child until you have calmed down yourself.

- Talk to the child about what happened. Allow the child the opportunity to tell what happened from her point of view. Do not interrupt or allow others to interrupt this explanation. The child has the right to be heard. Then reply by reflecting your understanding of the immediate trigger: 'You were very upset that Bob took your toy train without asking.'

- As far as you are able, backtrack to any other triggers that may have contributed to the meltdown: 'And it was a rainy day, and your socks were wet and I know you hate that.'

- Once the child has an understanding that you are being fair and that you are trying to understand her side, then she will be much more willing to listen to what you say next.

- Then lead the child to an understanding of other people's actions: 'Bob didn't know the train was yours. He got hurt when you hit him over the head with the train.'

- Explain again the classroom or home rules and how they protect everyone: 'And when the teacher saw you hit Bob, she yelled at you to stop because it is her duty to protect all the children. If someone hit you like that she would have yelled at the other person to stop too.' Then explore with the child alternative ways the situation could have been handled: 'Next time someone takes your toy, ask politely for it back. If that does not work, ask an adult for help.'

- Role-play the situation with a positive ending, or write social stories.

- Explain again about the safe place the child can go to if she feels her anger building up.

- Point out the child's triggers and help her see how she could have helped her situation earlier. Say things like, 'If you told the teacher that your socks were wet she would have let you take them off', 'Perhaps it's best not to take your own special toys to school', 'If you share your toys then you can enjoy playing with others.'

- If a punishment is called for (and don't forget, often the meltdown is punishment enough), a genuine *specific* apology might be enough: 'I am sorry I hit you on the head with my train, and that you got hurt.' If it is a repetitive problem, then the punishment must be relevant. Not allowing the child to bring his own toys to school is a more effective punishment, or rather solution, than 20 lines saying 'I must not hit Bob.'

- However, even better than punishment, a positive reward system is much more effective. If the child goes a whole week without hitting anyone, then she gets an extra long play session alone with the classroom train set.

- If meltdowns are a result of the child being bullied, then this must be taken very seriously and both the bullied and the bully must be spoken to so the bullying does not continue. The home and school *must* foster an environment where every child is safe. (See **Bullying**.)

- A child may become depressed when having to face the consequences of meltdowns and her inability to control emotions and environments. Depression must be taken seriously and, if necessary, professional help should be sought.

• If meltdowns keep on occurring when all has been done to alleviate them, keep a detailed diary of events of the day, such as daily routines or changes to routines. Think of all the senses, then track them through the day: the sound of school bells, work going on next door, smells that waft through the classroom, classroom temperatures and humidity, food the child eats. Write down anything you think could have been a trigger, regardless of how unlikely it seems. Then take all this information to a paediatrician or specialist and ask for advice.

Classroom activity

Always seek permission from the parents of the child with Asperger's before doing any activity to help the class to understand the child better.

• Have all the children in the classroom slip a piece of sandpaper somewhere under their clothes where it rubs against skin: in a collar, in a sock. Get them to sit on a small book so that they are sitting evenly. Play a repetitive annoying sound, such as a scratch on chalk-board. Have the teacher carry a small water pistol and squirt a child when they are not expecting it, or blow bubbles around the room. If possible, bring in a disco light, or get someone to stand at the lights and turn them on and off repeatedly. All the while, expect the children to learn something new, like a few words in a different language. After a few minutes, test what they learned. Now 'punish' those children who did not get 100 per cent by telling them they are lazy.

Then discuss how they felt and how hard it was to concentrate and how unjust your comments were. Brainstorm the problems that might come with having to put up with overwhelming sensory input all day. Talk about how easy it would be to snap at someone or get irritated and upset. Consider how coping with many overwhelming things can cause a meltdown. Discuss what would have helped them concentrate better. Discuss how they could have helped control their own environment (earphones, move away from others, go to a quiet place). Help them see that these issues are faced every day by people with Asperger's.

Home link

- Always inform the parents when a meltdown has occurred at school, giving as detailed a background as you can of the steps leading to the meltdown.

- Ask parents about any home problems or changes that may have influenced the build-up to the meltdown.

- If the child has had a bad day at school which included a meltdown, then encourage the parents to give her support and love at home so she has a safe place to retreat to away from the demands of peer pressure and social obligations.

- Never forget, when you speak to parents, that they love their children and want the best for them. Be respectful of the child regardless of her behaviour and assure parents of your support and willingness to work out a solution together.

Special Interests

Description

People with Asperger's often have an area of special interest in which they are happy to spend many hours researching and investigating. They develop a one-track mind and their interest becomes more than a hobby and can consume their time and dominate their conversations. Using the special interest in the classroom is a wonderful opportunity for the teacher to concentrate on the strengths of Asperger's rather than the weaknesses.

The child:

- becomes an expert in an area of interest, such as dinosaurs or train schedules, and can speak incessantly on this interest area to anyone who will listen and even to those who have stopped listening

- may be calmed and have anxiety reduced when working on a special interest

- may be able to overcome a fear of something by making it into a special interest and learning facts and knowledge to help understand the fear; for example, fear of spiders may lead to a special interest in arachnids

- is interested in things that interest his and is not usually influenced by current fads and phases of peers

- may be known as a 'little professor' or a genius when it comes to his special interest, but often does not take that skill set or interest of learning into other areas of school work; he may have an uneven report card with an A in the interest area but low scores and even failures in other subject areas

- may develop his interest area into a successful career as an adult

- may not adapt his special interest with age; for example, may still love Thomas the Tank Engine into teen years

- may have a strong attachment to an inanimate object involved with the special interest and takes it everywhere; its loss or disappearance can cause considerable distress

- may be more interested in a part of an object than the whole thing; for example, may be fixated on the motor of a Lego crane but not on the crane, or the wheel of the toy car rather than the car

- when play-acting, may prefer to become an object rather than a character; for example, would prefer to dress as a train than Superman, or as a tree than Robin Hood

- may use the special interest as a conversation starter, genuinely wanting the other person to feel the joy he does, not realizing that the other person may not be interested in the topic

- may interrupt others' conversations to speak about his interests.

HOW YOUR STUDENT MAY EXPLAIN IT

☼ People tell me my obsession with arranging my shell collection is strange. But I don't think it's strange. It makes me feel alive and energized and real. The intense joy I feel when I bring order to my shells is obviously something they have never experienced. I feel sorry for them.

☼ When my mind spins with thoughts and worries and sights and sounds, recording weather patterns calms me. I am in control and my mind clears up and my tensions drain away. I am now in a predictable world and things make sense.

☼ Life drains me. Coping with people drains me. Schools exhaust me. But when I play my computer games I get filled up again with energy and interest. I come alive. I can focus forever. I don't want to eat or sleep or even go to the bathroom. I hate being interrupted. When I am stopped, it's like peace and the beauty of order and control is snatched from me. Sometimes I admit I am not very nice to the person who takes this away from me. Would you be?

At school

- When a child with Asperger's gets a special interest, he becomes incredibly knowledgeable about that area. Use this knowledge, and the skills that come with it, to build self-esteem in the classroom and channel the interests into productive situations. For example, a child who loves lining up objects can be in charge of sorting and tidying the art room; the child who loves train timetables can help write the class rosters.

- Use the special interest to expand the child's knowledge base and skills. For example, get the child to use the library system to find resources on the topic; interview an adult who is an expert in the special interest area; make clay models; read books; write a story or poem or song about it; create a play; draw it; photograph it; make birthday cards depicting it. Be inventive!

- Give opportunities for the child to present his special interest to the class. Let him be the teacher for that lesson. This is a great opportunity to develop skills such as speaking slowly and clearly, keeping to time guidelines, preparing slides, encouraging eye contact with the audience, answering questions, and so on.

- If the subject is school-related, such as electricity, then have the child invited as a guest speaker to other classrooms.

- Be aware that special interests in computers or computer games and online gaming can potentially mean the child is able to get all his socializing needs through the internet. Limit this interest in a school situation and encourage social skills with 'real' people. On the flip side, other children interested in the same thing may value the child's skill in these areas. A balance is needed between building up the special interest areas and promoting life skills needed to survive in this world.

- Use the special interest as a reward to motivate the completion of other work. For example, give five minutes' free time on the computer if he finishes work on time.

- Set a clear boundary for when the special interest may be used or talked about. If the child knows that school work must be completed satisfactorily before he can read a favourite book, or that the toy dinosaur can be played with at lunch-time but not during class work, then the child is more likely to comply. It also helps the child know that the special interest is perfectly acceptable in the right time and place.

- Gather items in the special interest area that can be manipulated for maths or writing; for example, sets of plastic dinosaurs/small cars/shells/rocks to be sorted, counted, compared and be made into stories.

- Teach the child turn-taking when it comes to conversations. Say 'You can tell me about what interests you, and then I will tell you about something that interests me.' Timing a conversation can be beneficial: 'You have two minutes to tell me about the 46th matchbox toy you bought yesterday.' In class discussions, use a conversation ball; only the person holding the ball can talk. Again, if necessary, limit each conversation to a few minutes.

- Teach body language. Point out, 'When Mary was looking out the window when you talked, it meant that she wasn't listening and you should stop telling her about internal combustion engines.'

- There are times when bluntness is necessary to stop a child speaking on a special interest. If this is done firmly but gently, the child will not be offended, especially if he then knows exactly what you want him to do rather than having to try to guess what is required. For example, say 'Billy, I am sorry, but I do not have time to listen to you speak about coins any more. I have twenty other children who want to talk to me too.' Never wave the child away and say 'Not now, Billy.' Billy would then go away wondering when a good time would be or, more likely, would wonder what 'now' was not a good time for.

- Encourage the child to join a club with children of similar interests. Chess clubs or science clubs are very popular at schools. If no club exists, then help the child to start one.

- Use special interests to encourage participation in other subject areas. Use a Star Trek problem in maths. Have the child research the background of one of the records in the *Guinness Book of Records*. If rainfall is the special interest, then link this with plant growth or road system design. Be creative and enthusiastic. The child is much more likely to be excited about a link if you show enthusiasm too.

- Encourage the child to participate in many different activities. The child may be surprised at what suddenly becomes an interest. For example, he may hate sports day, but then realize that running the long-distance race felt good. Running could then develop into a special interest that is valued by peers, good for the health and a possible career path as an athlete or trainer.

- Often a child with an intense special interest will talk about it in inappropriate ways, such as going up to a stranger and talking about light bulbs or interrupting the flow of a conversation or class discussion with irrelevant facts. Calmly remind the child that there are times and places for his interests. Explain when he can and can't talk on that topic. Remind the child what is the present topic of conversation and invite him to participate.

- Remember that time spent on a special interest is a relaxing, calming time for the child. Where possible and appropriate, allow the child access to this interest.

- And above all, enjoy the child's bright intelligent mind.

Classroom activity

- Allow opportunities for the special interest to be incorporated in the classroom in a way that builds up self-esteem and peer acceptance. Have the child give a presentation on the special interest. Make him a guest speaker on parents' day or in another classroom. Allow the child to tutor younger children in the area. Basically, value the special interest and the child will feel valued.

Home link

- Explain to parents that when a child has a special interest, it can become entwined with his identity. To reject the special interest is effectively rejecting the child. Encourage the parents to value the special interest and show interest in it, ask about it, and help the child to develop and expand it. Help the child to present the special interest to his extended family and friends. Take the child on relevant excursions. By acknowledging the importance of the special interest to the child, parents can open doors of communication and improve his relationships.

- Explain to parents that special interests in children can be directed into areas of future employment as an adult. Many children on the spectrum are natural engineers or scientists or computer experts. Encourage the parents to work on directing an interest to a valid and desirable job prospect. If a child has a special interest that is not valued by others, or does not help in passing school subjects and does not lead itself to gainful employment (e.g. memorizing train schedules or the temperature fluctuations in the local area), then prompt the child to an area of strength that can be useful or is valued by others.

- Suggest that parents use the interest area as a reward for doing an activity that will develop him more socially; for example, he can play a computer game after a tennis lesson.

- Encourage parents to seek ways to support a special interest while developing ways to stretch the child beyond his comfort zone and to develop social skills and interests that help him grow as an individual. Help them see that giving in to a fixation may be an easy quick fix for a bit of peace, but will not help the child grow into a well-rounded adult.

Bullying

Description

Bullying is not always easy to define. What one person regards as bullying, another may regard as harmless play. However, the bullied person usually feels intimidated, distressed, helpless, and often is physically and emotionally harmed over a sustained period of time. Children with Asperger's are particularly vulnerable to bullying as they cannot read body language, do not understand sarcasm, and find it difficult to read others' intentions and often can't tell the difference between someone being friendly and someone trying to hurt them. Children who are being bullied do not always tell their parents or teachers simply because they are not aware it is something that can be changed. They can presume that bullying is just another part of the confusing tapestry of the neurotypical world. A teacher's role is to recognize and prevent bullying for all students and be especially vigilant on behalf of the child with Asperger Syndrome.

The bullied child may:

- experience physical and emotional trauma at the hands of others

- have her possessions damaged or stolen

- be called derogatory names or be confronted by derogatory gestures

- be shunned by peers

- have malicious rumours spread about her

- be a victim of cyber-bullying

- be manipulated into breaking rules and then left to take the consequences

- mimic the bullying behaviour of others, not realizing that those behaviours are unacceptable

- be lulled into a sense of friendship by others and then tricked into a situation where she is harmed; for example, is offered something nice to eat that has been spiked with chilli

- be provoked until she over-reacts and then others laugh at the resulting tantrum or meltdown

- avoid going to the place where bullying occurs

- avoid going to the toilet or other places at school where there are no cameras or adults

- do poorly in the class in which she is bullied or at school work generally

- begin to believe the horrible things said about her and become depressed or anxious and have a low self-esteem which can lead to clinical depression

- not forgive or forget easily and may replay the bullying episode over and over in her mind until it is resolved or explained

- often go to the help of another child who is being bullied

- have difficulties sleeping

- plan revenge on repeated attackers

- turn her special interest areas into self-protection or weapons

- need professional counselling to overcome the negative effects of sustained bullying

- in extreme cases, attempt suicide.

HOW YOUR STUDENT MAY EXPLAIN IT

☼ No one thing was the worst. It wasn't the name calling, it wasn't the punching, it wasn't the rock throwing, it wasn't my things being stolen and destroyed. It wasn't even the loneliness of being excluded from games and parties and friends. It was the unending, soul-destroying relentlessness of it all. They never ran out of ways to hurt me. Every day, day after day after day after day – a new way to crush me, to hurt me, to alienate me. Their inventiveness was amazing.

☼ Years later I still do not want to talk about it. It's still too painful and raw. I remember every bruise, every kick, every concussion, every contorted face sneering at me. The physical abuse was the least of it. The emotional torture was the worst. I lived in constant, dreadful fear, never knowing when or where the next attack would come.

☼ It was all my fault. I deserved the kicks and being spat on and my broken arm and my ripped clothes and my lunch being trodden on. It was my fault because I was different. I brought it on myself for not fitting in. That's what my teacher said when I complained. It was my fault.

☼ I was short. I was clumsy. I was very good at maths and useless at English. I had Asperger's. I never had a chance.

At school

Due to their difficulties with understanding social and cultural norms, many children with Asperger's are victims of sustained, vicious bullying by other children. *Do not* foster an environment where bullying is allowed. It is essential for the wellbeing of all students that the school has an anti-bullying policy that is rigorously upheld by all staff.

Here are some ways of dealing with bullying:

- Teachers play a vital role in setting the boundaries of respect for fellow students in a classroom situation. Be very careful that you, the teacher, do not become the class bully. Never ridicule or belittle a child with Asperger's, or any child for that matter. Don't use sarcasm or yell at a child or mimic her behaviours in a negative way. Do not use your body in a threatening way by clenching your fists or squinting your eyes, or towering over the child. All these things give the other children in the class a licence to do the same thing and can cause a caustic environment where the tormented and humiliated child can be scarred for life. All children should be able to trust that the teacher is there to protect them and to keep order and to foster an atmosphere of respect for others' differences.

- *Listen and be fair!* Others can easily manipulate your student into breaking rules and then leave her to face the punishment alone. It is pointless to simply ask the child with Asperger's 'Did you do this?' because most likely she will be honest and say 'Yes.' But that is not a full answer. Take the time to question her further, especially with the intention to find out if she was manipulated and if others were involved. Give her the benefit of the doubt. Ask other unbiased children for their version of the events. Question children separately so the child with Asperger's is not intimidated into being silent. And if punishment is warranted, be as fair as possible. The person who manipulates another into breaking the rules is just as guilty as the rule-breaker. (See **Classroom Discipline: To Punish or Not to Punish**.)

- Telling the child with Asperger's to ignore the taunts and tactics of bullying is not helpful. In an adult world, if your boss or peer constantly called you derogatory names, or menaced you physically, then you would have access to laws that would protect you. Children deserve the same rights. *You* are the law that protects them. Allow them to freely report when they are harassed or afraid and stop the bullying immediately.

- Explain to the child that when a bully teases and tries to get a reaction from the child then if the child reacts, it is playing into the hands of the bully. Explain that rather than ignoring the bully, or immediately going and telling a teacher, it is best to try to dismiss the teasing in a way that tells the bully that her comment is rather childish or lame or unoriginal. The child can roll her eyes and shrug and say things like, 'Was that supposed to be funny?', 'Did you think that up yourself?', 'Whatever.' However, this tactic must be monitored, as sometimes all this does is encourage the bully to 'step up the game'.

- Never dismiss a complaint of bullying with the old adage 'Kids will be kids' or 'Kids are cruel at this age, but they get over it.' To ignore behaviour in children (hair pulling, rock throwing, verbal assault) that would be a criminal offence in the adult world is a reckless denial of your responsibilities as a teacher.

- Occasionally, the child with Asperger's becomes the bully herself by yelling and kicking when she does not get her own way; by fighting others when upset; by being rough in showing affection, for example punching arms to show friendship; or by trying to force others to her way of thinking. Often the child genuinely has no idea that these behaviours are unacceptable. The simplest way to stop the behaviours is to gently, but firmly, point out how harmful they are. Once the Asperger child realizes she is breaking school rules, very often the behaviours stop quickly. If not, then be very clear on the punishments for continued misdemeanours and be fair and consistent in implementing the punishments.

- One of the greatest weapons against bullying is good self-esteem. If your student feels valued and accepted by you then she will believe she is a worthy person and if taunted or degraded by others will not so easily fall into the trap of believing she deserves it. Build up your students. Point out their strengths. Be liberal with praise. Laugh with them. Encourage your students to encourage and support each other. A warm, positive atmosphere is much less likely to foster bullying than a negative one.

- Make class rules clear and the punishment for breaking them even clearer. If a child with Asperger's feels she is getting an undeserved and unexpected punishment she will argue hard and long (and for a long time after it happens) and may have a tantrum or even go into a meltdown. If it is written on a chart that punching another student means three afternoons of detention, and a child with Asperger's punches another student, even if provoked, she will be likely to accept the detention. If a teacher suddenly says without warning, 'Right, for punching Tom, you will not get to go to your computer class this afternoon' then the child will be understandably confused and upset and will react badly.

- Be very careful to ensure that talking about bullying to your class does not give the bully more ammunition on how to bully. Never focus on the child who is actually bullied, but rather be generic in giving advice on what constitutes bullying, how to avoid it and how to report it.

- Never allow the other children in your class to be in a policeman role over others. If another child tells on the child with Asperger's for breaking minor rules, say politely 'You are not the teacher. It is not your job to make sure Jimmy behaves.' Likewise, if the Asperger child keeps telling the teachers of others' misdemeanours, say the same thing. As soon as you allow any child control over her peers, then you are at risk of creating an environment where bullying is allowed to fester.

- Be aware of the sneaky child. There is at least one in every class. This is the sly pincher, the tripper, the 'accidental' bumper, the one with a cruel tongue and an innocent smile. Being socially blind, body language blind, and unable to pick up on sarcasm, the child with Asperger's can be picked on mercilessly. The sneaky child also knows exactly how to upset a child with Asperger's and can do so day in and day out. However, when the Asperger child erupts in anger and lashes out in frustration, the sneaky child can quite rightly say 'All I did was accidentally bump his table, sir, and he punched me!' Often, the child with Asperger's is punished for over-reacting. Teacher, open your eyes. See what is behind a sudden burst of Asperger anger. Perhaps you'd do worse if the constant tormenting happened to you.

- Alternatively, the child with Asperger's, being naïve and trusting, may be lulled into forming a 'friendship' with her tormentors, often led by the sneaky child or the class bully, where she is the butt of the group's jokes but does not really understand what is going on. If you see this happening, stop the bullying immediately. Later, take the child aside and explain to her the real situation. 'When Bill asks if you want a soft drink, and then tips it into your hand when you say "Yes", you do not have to laugh when he laughs. He was not being funny; he was being mean.'

- One form of emotional bullying that is common for children with Asperger's is to be called stupid, gay, crazy, retard, and so on. The terms used by the bully (and sometimes by the teachers themselves) may seem relatively mild, and commonly bandied about in a classroom. However, anything that belittles an Asperger child's intelligence is particularly wounding as she prides herself on her intellect. Once bullies know that a term offends, they will use it at every opportunity just to watch the reaction. If you see this happening, ban the word in your class. On the other hand, children with Asperger's thrive when they are regarded as clever or wise. Teachers, use your words carefully!

- Some children who are bullied may over-react to perceived bullying and physically harm another child who may have said or done something the child finds disagreeable. In this case, talk to the child and rate each misdemeanour out of 10. For example, calling someone a retard may be ranked as 3 out of 10; hitting someone with a baseball bat would be ranked 10 out of 10. Help the child to see that to hit someone with a baseball bat when he calls you a retard is an uneven reaction.

- Try to create situations so the Asperger child will not be alone. Bullies love to attack the loners. Unfortunately, exclusion in the playground from other children's games and friendship groups is common. Encourage others in the class to accept the child into their groups. Organize a buddy system with a child in a higher grade to look out for her. Perhaps set up an activity group at lunch-times where the child with Asperger's can lead others in her interest area, for example chess or science or computers. Allow access to the library, which is a safe haven for isolated children where they can pursue their interests under the eye of a supervising adult.

- If you know your student is being bullied in situations out of your control, then help the child create a bully map. Write down the times and places where she is being bullied. See if there are ways to change a routine to avoid these places, or at least avoid being alone at those times. Help the child to report the bullying to the proper authorities. If appropriate, make parents aware of the situation so that they can help.

- Exclusion from class activities is very humiliating and often no one wants the Asperger child in their group. Always prearrange groups and sporting activities so that all children are allocated to set groups so that the Asperger child is not put in the position of always being the last one chosen.

- Offer a self-defence course at the school so that the child can learn to stay calm in a crisis and have greater confidence in her ability to defend herself.

- Be aware of cyber-bullying. This may not happen directly at school, but may severely impact the child in your class. It is where the child is taunted, ridiculed or harassed on social media. Her own sites may be bombarded with cruel and hurtful messages. Videos or images of the child in embarrassing situations, such as being physically or sexually harassed, may be uploaded for all to see. This means that the child cannot escape the bullying, not even in the safety of the classroom or home. Cyber-bullying is hideously endemic and the consequences of such exposure can be devastating to any child, let alone the vulnerable child with Asperger's. To help prevent cyber-bullying, put in place a school-wide policy on zero tolerance, making sure all students know that to cyber-bully means severe punishment and even expulsion.

Encourage students to limit access by others to their sites and never to give out personal details such as phone numbers or addresses online. Encourage students to report all cases of cyber-bullying immediately.

- Some children with Asperger's may be manipulated by false friends into misusing the internet to download pornography or to hack into others' sites. They do so innocently, thinking they are just being helpful, and may not fully understand the implications of such things. Try to prevent this by discussing it in class and stressing that such activities are wrong and illegal even if a 'friend' asks for it. If the child is still manipulated, then be sure that both the child and manipulator are equally punished and the child with Asperger's has her actions clearly explained as wrong.

- Seek the help of specialist staff in the school, or discuss with parents the possible need to seek outside professional advice to help the child gain the skills to deal with the situation.

Classroom activity

It is important not to single out the child with Asperger's when trying to deal with bullying in the classroom. If you do, it may give the bullies more ammunition on how to bully. However, by giving general awareness of the problem, then the Asperger child may learn some tips on how to cope.

- Arrange the desks in a room to form a simple maze. Put the children into a group, and they select one person to be maze navigator and others will be the support team. Blindfold the maze navigator and then her support team will shout out directions so she can get through the maze. The first time round, they cry out negative things like, 'No stupid, don't go that way.' Or, 'Are you deaf? I said *right*.' Keep insults within decorum. If you don't trust your class to be sensible, then call out the comments yourself. Next time round, encourage the maze navigator with positive comments: 'Excellent, you turned right in time' or 'Brilliant stuff, you are almost there!'

Then discuss with the navigators how they felt at the different times and promote the concept that behaving positively towards others can yield positive reactions.

Home link

- Explain the school's bullying policy to parents, and assure them of the school's full support for their child in cases of bullying.

- Explain that often a child will not tell parents, carers or teachers about bullying. However, some warning signs the carers can watch out for are:

    ○ asking for money to take to school

    ○ not wanting to go to school

    ○ feeling sick each morning before school

    ○ a drop in grades

    ○ coming home with ripped clothes, missing items, unexplained bruises

    ○ increase in anxiety, sadness, depression

    ○ withdrawal from family and friends

    ○ bedwetting

    ○ not sleeping well

    ○ an increase in aggression at home

    ○ getting upset after receiving a phone call or text or going onto the computer

    ○ talking about herself in a negative way.

- Encourage the carers to listen to the child calmly and to make a plan together to combat the problem. The child must feel

that the carers are on her side and not feel she is to blame in some way for being a victim.

- If a child is very upset one day about a bullying incident at school, write up what happened in a class diary that goes between home and school so the child does not have to try to explain every step again to her parents and carers.

- Discuss with parents the strategies that you use to combat bullying and listen to their ideas as well.

- Be sensitive to the possibility that some parents are unsympathetic to a child's school problems. In this case, use discretion when getting such parents involved in a school incident.

- Keep a library of 'bullying books' that you can loan to parents to help them with bullying that may be occurring to their child in places outside your control.

- If physical bullying is a major problem, suggest to parents the possibility of enrolling their child in a course of self-defence, or martial arts, so she can learn to protect herself if necessary and learn to stay calm in a crisis.

- Suggest that parents encourage the child in areas that she excels in to build up self-esteem and confidence.

- Strongly advise the parents not to try to take matters into their own hands or to contact the bully directly. Help them to go through the correct channel, that is, through the school, to come to a resolution.

Field Trips, Excursions and Camps

 Field trips, excursions and camps cause a major disruption in the life of a child with Asperger Syndrome. They take the child to a new place, with new rules and sights and sounds and smells and experiences and expectations. They break a comforting routine and may force a child to mix with new or unknown people. The excursion may expose the child to situations so beyond his ability to cope that it becomes a living nightmare. However, it does not have to be this way. With forethought, planning and understanding, it is quite possible for the child to enjoy these trips.

Before the trip

- Long before the trip, inform the class and caregivers about the excursion. Paste an image of the place you are visiting on the class calendar.

- Show pictures, videos, YouTube clips, books, and so on about the place to be visited.

- Give the big picture. For example, if visiting a museum, say, then show on a map where it is situated and perhaps even the route the bus will take to get there. Explain how long the trip will take, when you will leave, when you will eat there, when you will return. Explain that times are variable, and rather than say we leave at 8.00am, say we leave between 8.00am and 8.10am and will return between 2.30pm and 2.40pm. Explain why you are going there and what the children will be expected to do. If a follow-up assignment is to be completed, explain that thoroughly before you go.

- Hand out a programme sheet to outline what will happen while there and, as far as possible, adhere to the schedule.

- Reassure the child that an adult will be close by at all times to answer any questions.

- If possible, and if necessary, allow caregivers to come on the excursion.

- If you, or the child's parents, feel that this excursion is beyond the child's ability to cope then it may be prudent to allow the child to miss the excursion.

When you arrive

- Orientate the class. Point out the direction you just came from. Show on a map where they now are. Show where relevant places are: toilets, eating areas, and so on.

- Explain where you and other adult helpers will be.

- Show a safe place they can go if they get lost or need to ask questions; for example, the information desk in a museum.

- If doing field work, encourage the children to draw pictures of what they see, or write answers to questions as they go. Collect brochures and other materials that can be cut up and used for assignment work later. Having something specific to focus on can help the Asperger child overcome the sensory and disorientating issues he is facing.

- If staying overnight, talk about the new sounds they might hear. Suggest that the child with Asperger's wears a hat to bed to help muffle sounds. Be sure he knows what to do if feeling unsafe. Show him where the closest adult is sleeping. Perhaps allow him to have a mobile phone with an emergency number on speed dial. If possible, and if necessary, allow the child to sleep with his own caregiver.

- If staying in group accommodation, such as a cabin or tent, be sure to put the child in with other children who are kind and accepting.

Sensory issues on a field trip

Be aware that many children with Asperger's have sensory issues that can be magnified on a class trip. Take the child's complaints seriously even if they seem petty. The child is not trying to be difficult. He has genuine and often severe issues to deal with and deserves to be heard and helped. Here are some issues with suggestions for how to deal with them:

- Many children with Asperger's are prone to travel sickness. If this is the case with your student, then allow the child to sit at the front of the bus or where he feels most comfortable. Motion sickness can even be felt on escalators or lifts, so watch the child carefully in these situations.

- Do not force the child into an overcrowded seat where other children are pressed up against him. It may be best if the child is seated next to an adult.

- Some children may be very sensitive to the sun, so allow them to sit on the shady side of the vehicle or sit in the shade to eat. Direct sun can really hurt, and glare from roads and water can be unbearable. Allow the child to wear a hat and sunglasses at all times, even indoors.

- The noise on a bus can be very loud. Encourage the use of earphones so the child can listen to calming music. Allow the child to pull a cap hard over his ears to block sounds.

- Children with body awareness and balance issues may find it difficult to walk on uneven surfaces or to go up and down stairs and road kerbs, especially in unfamiliar places. If age-appropriate, hold the child's hand. Otherwise, watch the child carefully. Encourage the holding of rails. Or simply walk close to the child and be there in case he overbalances.

- Allow the child to bring his own food on the trip.

- Encourage the child to bring a tactile or stress toy to fiddle with to help relieve stress. For the younger child this can be an obvious object like a doll or strip of material. For the older child, something as simple as a pebble in a pocket he can fiddle with can work wonders.

- If the child has a favourite smell that calms him, bring that in a small bottle or on a handkerchief so that it can be sniffed unobtrusively.

- Some children with balance (vestibular system) issues may have difficulties walking around in the dark as they get very disorientated. If camping, or staying overnight, be sure that the child has a torch close by so he can get up safely if he has to.

After the trip

- Discuss what was fun and what was not.

- Praise the child for things he coped with and did well. Talk about times when things may have not gone so well. Discuss or play-act ways things could have gone better.

- Make a journal of the trip to help the child remember relevant details.

- Make up a plan of what could help next time to make the trip even better.

Homework

Description

The chances are that you will not long have a child with Asperger's in your classroom before the issue of homework raises its head. There seem to be some sort of polar opposites built into the child and the homework that repel each other. There is no one reason why this is so, but at its simplest, the child knows she has to work all day on school work at school, because that makes sense. *School* work at school, right. But school work at *home*...it's not logical.

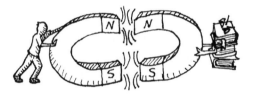

Also, the child has to expend an enormous amount of energy just to survive in the average classroom. Not only does she have to contend with the scholastic curriculum, but the child also has to cope with an influx of a myriad of sensory blasts from noises, sounds, tastes, smells and sights. Add to all that, the child has to navigate a social minefield, never being quite sure exactly when a given situation will explode. No wonder when she gets home, all the child wants to do is relax alone, preferably immersed in a special interest. Homework? Forget it.

However, it is an unfortunate truth that in almost every school in the world, homework is a given, even for children as young as four and five. As a teacher, unless you have the power to veto this, you will be expected to give homework to your student with Asperger's, and to grade it accordingly. By its very nature, homework is not exactly a classroom consideration, but it will impact your student considerably so everything that you can do to ease the situation will be hugely appreciated by the students, parents and carers alike. The good news is that there are many ways that you can help your student hand in that dreaded homework. (See **Organizing Your Student to be Organized: Executive Functioning**.)

HOW YOUR STUDENT MAY EXPLAIN IT

💡 I can't find my pencil. I don't know where my stupid books are. I don't know what I have to do. I don't know how to do it. I don't understand why I have to sit here. I am hungry. I am thirsty. I am angry. I hit the things off my desk. I kick the table leg over and over. I look out the window. I hum. I tap. This is stupid. This is homework.

At school

- Avoid asking the class to copy the homework directly from the board. That simple task alone can be quite stressful for the child with Asperger's as she may copy incorrectly, or not get time to copy all the work down before the class finishes. Rather, hand out the homework on a sheet and underline clearly which section the child needs to complete that night. Glue this into a class diary that the child takes to and from school each day. The class diary should also include which subjects will be addressed on a given day and which books need to be taken for each class. It can also be used as a communication tool between parents and the teacher. An alternative to a hand-out sheet could be to email the homework or otherwise electronically transfer it in some way. Many schools are starting to use internal websites exactly for this sort of use.

- Another fun way to send homework home could be to dictate it into a digital recorder or the child's phone. The child may be quite excited to use a gimmick like that, and the parents can get a clear description of what you want done.

- However you send it home, beside each section of the homework, write (or speak) the approximate amount of time you expect the child to spend completing it. That way, parents can contact you if the homework takes much longer than expected.

- If the homework is a long assignment, or an essay, sit with the child and formulate a plan for having it finished on time. Then mark, or at least review, each section as it is completed, to help the child know if she is on track. There is nothing worse than the child struggling for weeks at home only to fail because the original understanding was incorrect.

- Make sure the child with Asperger's, or the child's parents, have the contact details of another child in the class that she could call for clarification on a project. Even better, if you are comfortable with it, allow the child or the parents to call you directly after school hours to clarify homework issues.

- Where possible, incorporate the child's special interest in homework options. Let the child divide groups of Star Wars characters rather than blocks. Allow the research assignment to include train schedules. The parents will find it much easier to help the child with homework if it is work the child is happy to do.

- Where possible, allow time for the child to complete homework at school. If permitted, have an open-door policy in your classroom at lunch-time so the child can complete work then. Of course, an adult must be present while children are in any classroom. Alternatively, the child may go to the library. This has an added benefit of making sure the loner child is occupied and safe from bullying during lunch periods. Homework can also be completed if there is an opportunity for free time at the end of the day, or a free period. Perhaps you could start a homework 'club' at school where children are permitted to stay back for an hour after school each day under the supervision of a teacher for the express purpose of helping them complete homework.

- Homework should mostly be to consolidate facts learned on different subjects. It should never be a time where the child has to learn new things on her own.

- Give the child an incentive to complete homework while still in class time. For example, say to your class, 'Finish all page three, and what you don't finish in class will be your homework.' You may be amazed how fast your students work then!

- Avoid giving homework that has to be completed by the next day. So many children these days have after-school activities so it is impossible to know if every child in your class has the time and opportunity to complete work in one day. If possible, hand out homework sheets at the beginning of the week and allow all week to complete them.

- If homework is a major issue for all concerned, then consider asking the school authorities if the child can be exempted. Perhaps give it a month's trial. See if having the freedom to go home and relax each day rather than being forced to do homework actually improves the child's concentration and grades.

Home link

- Discuss with parents some ways in which they can help with the child's homework. Assure them of your support and willingness to work through this issue together.

- Explain to parents why homework is so hard for their child. Explain how hard the child has to work at school coping with not only the curriculum, but the social minefield and sensory onslaught as well. Help parents empathize with the exhausted child at the end of each day.

- Suggest that parents create a homework space where the child works at the same place each day.

Keep it clear from clutter and from distracting influences. Keep it safe from siblings who may mess up the child's 'system'. Make sure the TV cannot be seen from where the child sits, or that the television is turned off. Turn off disrupting music or, alternatively, turn on quiet background music to create a calm environment. Allow the child to wear earphones and have her own music going if that helps with blocking out other noises. If the homework does not involve the use of a computer, do not sit the child close to it. If the homework does involve the computer, then make sure the parent can see the screen with ease. Avoid noisy housework, such as vacuuming or mowing, while the child is working. Place only the items and books needed for the specific homework on the work space.

- One thing the child objects to is doing 'school' work at home. Ask the parents to consider calling 'homework' *study time*. Many children will try to avoid doing homework by saying that they don't have any, thus avoiding the routine for that night. However, the parent can come back and say 'You can still study at study time though. Go to your desk and read through yesterday's work for ten minutes.' It can be surprising how the child might miraculously remember a bit of homework she can do after all.

- Class diaries that go between teacher and parent are essential. Make sure the child has it updated before she leaves the class, and encourage the parent to make sure it is brought back to school the next day.

- Encourage parents to make a set time each day for the child to do homework. Make sure it does not clash with something the child loves, such as a certain TV show. It is best if the child is not hungry or thirsty or too tired or too hyperactive. Choose a time after the child is fed a snack, had a chance to unwind a bit by doing her favourite activity, and also had some physical activity such as a walk or run or sporting activity. Do not leave it too late at night or the child will legitimately be too tired to concentrate.

- Explain to parents that it may help to break the homework into small pieces. If the child has homework from different subjects, attack them one at a time. Set the child a task, and a time limit: 'Do the sums up to number 5 and you have ten minutes to finish them.' The parent should not hover or look over the child's shoulder all the time, but rather be close by and available so the child does not have the excuse to get up from her chair and go looking for help. Give warnings as the time passes. The parent can use a timer, or point out the hands on a clock: 'When the big hand reaches 8 you must have finished up to number 5.' It is best if the parent has a realistic expectation of how long each task will take, so make sure you provide this when you send the homework home.

- Give parents guidelines as to when it is appropriate to stop the homework even if it is not finished, for example: if the child is crying or overstressed; if the child honestly has no idea what to do; if the child takes much longer than the teacher guidelines mention. In these cases encourage the parent to write about the issue in the class diary, or to come and see you the next day.

- Explain to parents that the child with Asperger's often has great difficulties organizing herself with time management. Write up calendars for the child with due dates of upcoming assignments, excursions, sporting activities, exams and other relevant school activities. Help them see that if an assignment is due on Friday, and Wednesday and Thursday are busy with after-school activities, then really the assignment must be finished by Tuesday. Devise exam study timetables so the child is not forced to cram on two or three subjects on one night.

- Encourage the parents to be calm but firm. Don't shout at the child, or call the child lazy or stupid. Rather, say things like, 'You are a very clever boy. I know you can do this.' Parents or siblings can share the load of assisting the child in different subjects so that it is not just one person helping with homework every day. Perhaps Dad is the one who helps with maths and Mum is good at geography. An older sibling might be great at helping with computer studies. Likewise, the child with Asperger's might help someone else in the home with downloading apps. When the child can see that she does not have to cope with homework alone, then she is less likely to get stressed over it.

- Discuss with parents the possible need for a tutor, especially in a subject area that no one at home can help with. The tutor brings a new face and a lot of expertise that the child will most likely respect.

- Give parents some leeway on the completion of homework, preferably without the student knowing, or the child will play on this. Perhaps you can have a secret agreement with the parents that if the child is having a bad day, then she only has to do every second exercise. Or perhaps give an extension on the due date for an assignment. Perhaps, allow the child to dictate answers to the parent and the parent types them up.

- Remind parents to give the child realistic breaks after a reasonable amount of time: 'When you finish up to number 10 then you can take the dog for a walk around the block.'

- Reward the child with time on her special interest. However, warn the parents that to withhold the special interest unreasonably is the worst thing they can do. If the child knows that she will not get time on the computer then all her incentive to work is gone. It is better for the child to know that, every day, she is allowed from 4.30–5.00pm uninterrupted time to play games. As a bonus, if the child completes all her homework before 8.00pm that night, then she will get another half-hour.

- If the child is young, she may respond well to behaviour charts with smiley faces for work well done, or work done in the set time, or work done without complaining or whining. Ten smiley faces may allow the child to choose a treat such as a special food item or toy, or more time on a special interest.

Classroom Discipline

To Punish or Not to Punish

Description

One of the hardest roles for a teacher is to be a disciplinarian. With up to thirty children in a classroom and a curriculum to teach, it is important that you have control of the students so that they can learn. Whole books have been written on classroom management, and there are numerous techniques that can be applied. However, this chapter will deal specifically with discipline issues related to children with Asperger Syndrome.

In essence, when it comes to disciplining a child with Asperger's, the best motto to follow is:

Be fair. Be consistent. Be fair.

HOW YOUR STUDENT MAY EXPLAIN IT

- ♀ I am always getting into trouble for not making eye contact. One teacher came right up to my face and pressed his forehead against mine and screamed at me to look at him. I remember that day twenty years later. Each time I remember, it is as bad as the day it happened.

- ♀ I got punished all the time, but never knew why. I don't think the teachers liked the way I breathed.

- ♀ I was in my fourth grade before I had a teacher who let me sit with the other kids. Every teacher before that made me sit by myself, telling me I was too naughty to mix with others. This teacher even seemed to like me. It was a good year.

At school

- Be careful that your own behaviour is not causing the child to appear to misbehave:

  ◦ If the child has not obeyed your instructions, such as to put his books away, perhaps you gave a general instruction to the class and the child did not realize it was also meant for him.

  ◦ Perhaps the child did not hear you as other noises, even ones you cannot hear, are louder to the child than your voice.

  ◦ Perhaps you did not get the child's attention first when you gave your instruction and the child was so engrossed in the present activity that he simply did not hear you.

  ◦ Perhaps you spoke too quickly and the child could not understand you.

  ◦ Perhaps you gave too many verbal instructions and the child could not comprehend or remember them all.

  ◦ Is the child in trouble for doing something that you let him get away with yesterday? If you are not consistent in enforcing a rule then you can't blame the child for breaking it.

  ◦ Are you angry and threatening, or sarcastic and demeaning? No child will react favourably to those things.

  ◦ Be sure to check your own behaviours and actions before accusing the child of misbehaviour.

- *Listen and be fair!* Others can easily manipulate your student into breaking rules and then leave him to face the punishment alone. It is pointless to simply ask the child with Asperger's 'Did you do this?' because most likely he will be honest and say 'Yes.' But that is not a full answer. Take the time to question him further, especially with the intention to find out if he was manipulated and if others were involved. Give him the benefit of the doubt. Ask other unbiased children for their version of the events. Question children separately so the child with Asperger's is not intimidated into being silent. And if punishment is warranted, be as fair as possible. The person who manipulates another into breaking the rules is just as guilty as the rule-breaker. (See **Bullying**.)

- Make sure that the class rules are known to all and preferably written down on a chart or on a hand-out sheet that goes home to parents. Go through the class rules so that every child not only knows what is acceptable and unacceptable, but also what are the likely repercussions if the rules are broken. Always stick to the repercussions and do not change them at whim or from child to child or from day to day.

- Even if you go to great lengths to make sure the rules are known to all the children in the class, do not presume that the Asperger child actually understands each rule and all its implications. Your rule might be 'Do not graffiti school walls', but the child may feel free to graffiti fences and be stunned when he gets into trouble for it. The child may have a short-term memory issue and although yesterday could recite a rule, today cannot remember it. He may know the rule 'Wash your paint brushes after use', but simply flicks the brush once under a running tap, not understanding that it was expected that all paint be washed from the bristles. Clarify that the child knows and understands a rule before punishing him for breaking it.

- Rewarding a child for good behaviour is much more effective than having to punish for bad behaviour. The most effective reward of all for a child with Asperger's is allowing him to have some time with his special interest. Be strict with timing so the child understands when his reward time is up. Set a time and say you may play on the computer for ten minutes but when the timer goes you must go back to your activity. Give a warning at the five-minute mark that half the time is up, and then again warn a minute before the end. Some timers allow for more than one setting, which is very useful in this situation.

- Avoid taking away the child's recess time. The child needs to be free to move and not be forced to sit still for another period. This is especially important if the child has body awareness issues. The child also may need to be alone and quiet during the recess in order to recharge and recover to be able to cope with the rest of the day.

- Recognize the child's individual needs and do not punish things the child does out of necessity. It is useless to punish a child with tactile issues for wriggling all the time if you are forcing him to sit on an itchy carpet. No matter how much you insist that the child pays attention, he cannot obey if the flickering of fluorescent lights is driving him crazy. Go beyond the bad behaviours to find the source. Be sure to ask the child why he is acting in a 'naughty' way before presuming that the child is truly naughty.

Classroom activity

Before doing this activity, stress that it is just a game and that no child will actually be punished. If you wish to relate this activity to the behaviour of a child in your class with Asperger's, make sure you have the permission of the child and the child's parent to do so.

- Inform the class that today you have a new rule (e.g. don't touch your nose or don't blink when talking to the teacher). Don't explain what the rule is, but inform the class that the punishment for breaking this secret rule will be to be kept in for five minutes after class. As each child breaks the rule, put his name on the board, but still don't explain what the rule is. If a child breaks the rule twice, pretend to get frustrated. If the child breaks it a third time, get angry. After a while, see if the class can guess what each child did 'wrong'.

Now explain how frustrating it is to be punished when you have no idea what you did wrong. Discuss how a natural reaction is to question what rule was broken, or deny doing anything wrong and argue against the punishment. Discuss how knowing the rule can change people's behaviour; or, at least, when they break the rule they can understand what punishment can be expected.

Explain how people with Asperger's often have no idea what rule they have broken and can get upset when disciplined. Help the class to understand that the Asperger child might also unknowingly break social rules such as barging into other people's conversations. In this case, rather than yelling at the child, or telling him to go away, explain first what 'rule' was broken and ask him not to do it again.

Home link

- Discuss with parents the ways you deal with discipline in the classroom. Share with each other ways that work best for the child.

- Explain how important it is for the parent to be fair, clear and consistent about rules, and be fair, clear and consistent with punishment.

- One punishment that a parent can use that is not applicable in the classroom is to use a fining system. If the child disobeys a rule (e.g. dumped his school bag in the middle of the stairs) then he might get fined a small amount of money. This amount can be as little as a few cents and still be effective. Alternatively, the child might be given a small amount of money each time he obeys the set rules each day. If the child goes a week without a fine he may get half an hour extra time of his special interest.

SENSORY ISSUES

Overview

Most people are aware of the five basic senses: sight, hearing, touch, taste and smell. However, there are two other senses not so well known: balance (vestibular system) and body awareness (proprioception).

Many children with Asperger Syndrome, but not all, have problems with their senses that can affect their lives in a profound way. Although pain comes under the umbrella of touch, it is considered here in its own right. Synaesthesia is another sensory issue considered where one sense may be interpreted by a different sense; for example, a colour may have a taste.

To have a sensory disorder is like having a faulty electrical connection. If you tap a faulty wire one way, it can spark. If you tap it in another direction, it turns off. Some children seem to have the 'switch' permanently wired in one direction and be either overloaded, that is, hypersensitive to input; or the child does not seem to get much input at all, that is, hyposensitive to input. However, the same wire can be wiggled to produce an array of results – spark, working okay, spark, off, working okay – all in a very short time. Likewise, a child with a sensory disorder may have a 'faulty' sensory system and within a short period of time can be overloaded with input and then seem immune to it. For example, she may cringe at a hug, then seek one later the same day. A small cut can cause excruciating pain, then the child skips away after a nasty fall causing gravel rash.

If you, as a teacher, think that this is confusing, then try being the child with a sensory disorder in a classroom. There, the child is bombarded with a maelstrom of sensory input: the smell of sweaty bodies, the noise of other children, the clacking of fans, the humming of air conditioners, the flicker of lights, the hardness of the seat, the itchiness of a uniform, the dizziness of being bumped, the pain of bumping into things…and all the while trying to concentrate on one person's voice at the front. Imagine how confusing life is for her!

To make things even more complex, sensory issues are aggravated or alleviated by how much sleep the child had the night before, her emotional state, the weather, her proximity to other children, bullying, how new her clothes are, how hungry or thirsty the child is, and a multitude of other factors which may never be known.

Tony Attwood, a clinical psychologist, explains it this way: Imagine that every mind is a clearing in a forest. In the middle of the clearing a tree begins to grow. For most children, this 'tree' in their mind represents their ability to socialize. As they grow older, their 'tree' grows bigger and bigger and forms a canopy under which there is shade. In this shade are their senses. In a classroom, their ability to behave socially appropriately is huge and they are able to block (shade) the input from their senses. They are able to conform to society's expectation to listen to a teacher and they can ignore the chattering outside the class, or the smell of the fried food from the canteen.

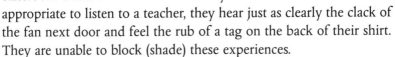

For a child with Asperger's, the tree is very small; just a bush or, in extreme cases, a flower. Their senses get full sun and thrive. So in a classroom situation where it is socially appropriate to listen to a teacher, they hear just as clearly the clack of the fan next door and feel the rub of a tag on the back of their shirt. They are unable to block (shade) these experiences.

So if a child suddenly displays unusual behaviours, consider what may have changed in the classroom or environment that her 'small tree' may not have been able to block out. For example, the child may have loved painting and then suddenly when the class starts sketching, she hates art. The reason may be that the sound of the pencil scratching on paper distresses her, or the smell of the sketching paper is different from that of the painting paper. Perhaps the child loved the tactile pleasure of washing the brushes, but now keeps snapping the pencil tips due to using the wrong pressure on the page. Or maybe the child is tired or it is a rainy day and the sound of raindrops is intensely annoying. There are so many possibilities to explain a child's behaviours.

On the bright side, if a sensory issue can be isolated and the offending input removed, then your 'naughty', restless child may miraculously become a model student. It is definitely worth the effort and time to try to understand and eliminate sensory problems for your student.

Hearing

Description

A child who has problems with his auditory system may be *hypersensitive* or *hyposensitive* to sound.

Hypersensitive means that the hearing system (auditory) is over-responsive and the child does not seek stimulation. The child:

- may hear noises that other people can't hear, including sounds outside the normal hearing frequency range, the noise of lights flickering, the whine from computers, conversations in another room, even the click-clack of butterfly wings!

- may complain that 'ordinary' sounds are too loud, and can find certain frequencies unbearable and may put his hands over his ears

- dislikes crowds and noisy environments, such as parties, movie theatres, concerts, skating rinks, fairs

- copes better in a situation where he is in control of the noise levels and may hate other people's noise, but then may make a lot of noise himself

- is startled and afraid and may cry or try to hide when sudden loud noises occur (e.g. fire alarms, dog barking, fireworks, even the toilet flushing)

- hates noisy machinery such as vacuum cleaners, blenders, lawn mowers

- may complain of sounds in his ears, such as ringing or hissing

- finds it difficult to separate important sounds (teacher talking) from unimportant sounds (fan clacking)

- may find it very difficult to follow oral directions, especially if there are more than two, and will often ask for things to be repeated

- finds it hard to focus on one sound amongst many (one person talking in a crowd) and may not be able to recognize the source of a sound

- may look to others for reassurance before speaking or answering a question

- can find accents very hard to understand and may not recognize even his own name if said in a different way; for example, Freddie may not respond to 'Friddie' or 'Fraddie'

- may like or dislike a person purely by the sound of their voice

- can be hyper-aware of the sounds of letters and can misunderstand meanings if the speaker does not speak clearly; for example, the child might hear 'if you're tall' instead of 'if at all', or 'a turtle' instead of 'eternal', thus causing the child to stop listening to what comes next because he is trying to make sense of what was just heard

- may find it difficult to read out loud

- can sometimes speak and listen more clearly after heavy exercise.

Hyposensitive means that the hearing system (auditory) is under-responsive and the child craves stimulation. The child:

- may prefer noisy situations, loud places, and plays TV or music very loudly

- may concentrate better in a noisy environment or with background noise such as a TV or radio playing, listening to music through earphones

- may sleep better with background noise, such as a fan or air conditioner being on, or a radio playing softly

- often does not respond to verbal instructions or hear his own name being called and seems not to hear some sounds at all

- will often ask for things to be repeated, and says 'What?' a lot

- likes to make a lot of noise of which he is in control

- can have a lot of trouble remembering or understanding what is said

- may not have babbled much as a baby.

HOW YOUR STUDENT MAY EXPLAIN IT

💡 No one understands what it is like to hear everything. The noise of an aeroplane flying over the school is as loud to me as the teacher's voice. The scrape of a chair is like an arrow piercing my brain. *'Listen!'* my teacher yells, and I can't explain that that is my problem. I listen too much.

💡 I simply cannot understand when people mumble their words or talk too quickly. All the sounds blend together because they don't bother to speak clearly, but I am the one who gets into trouble for not hearing their gibberish. Life really is not fair sometimes.

💡 Other people don't hear what I hear. The dripping of a tap sounds like a drum in my head and the hum of a light is so irritating that I can't concentrate. It's almost impossible to make others understand what it is like. I rub my ears to block out excruciating sounds and they think I'm weird.

At school

- Put yourself into the child's shoes. Imagine you had a cold and your hearing was poor, and you were trying to understand someone who has a heavy accent and speaks quickly. You would soon switch off or get frustrated trying hard to understand what was said. Likewise, if verbal input is too much and poorly heard and misunderstood by a child with auditory problems, he can switch off or get frustrated. And then if the child gets into trouble for asking for something to be repeated, or makes a mistake with instructions, then the child will understandably become upset and angry. If you are frustrated by the child's apparent misbehaviour, imagine how frustrated he is! Do not automatically jump to the conclusion of naughtiness if a child is disobeying you or not following instructions, but rather repeat instructions clearly and kindly, and allow the child to ask questions if necessary.

- If a child speaks out of turn, or makes a comment that is off topic, consider that he is not trying to be difficult, but rather may not have heard or understood the topic on hand and may not understand the rules of speaking in turn. Gently guide him to the correct way of interacting.

- Headphones and earplugs can help shut out unwanted noise. Try to find noise mufflers rather than ones that shut out all sound, so the child can still hear instructions. Be aware that some children may hate the tight sensation of the earphones or the feeling of objects pressed into their ears. Also be aware that constant use of earphones and earplugs can actually harm a child's hearing, so use with discretion and only with parental permission.

- Do not presume that the child will hear and/or understand general instructions said to a class. He may hear the words 'Sit up, everyone', but not realize that those instructions include him. Get the child's attention first by saying his name, or gently tapping the desk in front of him or tapping on his shoulder if the child does not mind touch. Alternatively, ring a little hand-bell, or make a consistent gentle sound to call everyone's attention to you. Then, only when you know the child is listening, give class instructions.

- Use a consistent phrase for a specific instruction. If you want the children to stop what they are doing and listen to you, then be specific. Say 'Stop and listen' rather than 'All eyes on me' or 'Right, next thing...'

- Remember that many children on the spectrum are visual learners. A child with auditory sensitivities relies even more heavily on visual clues. As well as speaking instructions, write them on the board or give out a sheet with the instructions listed. Use diagrams and visual clues, such as pointing to the left if you want the child to write his name on the left side of the paper. If giving verbal instructions, give no more than two at once. As well as giving spoken instructions, such as, 'Do up to exercise four in your work book', mark in the child's book where he has to stop.

- Use visual schedules in class so the child knows what to expect from the day. He is more likely to hear 'Time to clean up' if he can see on the daily schedule that art class finishes at 11am. Or he will know to get out maths books, even if he does not hear the instruction, if he knows that it's the next subject on the schedule.

- If a child has a set time to do a task, rather than just saying 'You now have 15 minutes to finish this', help him to track the time by using an egg-timer, or moving a small marker across the desk as the time passes, or showing hands on a clock.

- Speak slowly and clearly. Fast, blurred speech is very difficult for a child with auditory difficulties to understand.

- Give the child extra time to answer a question verbally as it can be difficult for him to process the question and then put an answer into words. Or give a warning that a response will be required. For example, instead of going through homework and randomly asking children their answers for certain questions, say to the child 'I will be asking you your answer to number 4.'

- Experiment with your class environment to see what helps the child best with his needs while acknowledging that other children in the class may have different needs; for example, expecting absolute silence all the time is not realistic. Try playing quiet music as the class works. Shut windows if outside noise is disruptive. Create workstations that are isolated from the body of the class and allow the child to go there whenever he wants to. Design a quiet corner or a place with pillows and very little clutter for the child to retreat to when feeling stressed. Hang earphones on the wall and allow any child access to them at will. Fluorescent lights give off a buzzing sound that many on the spectrum can hear, so if possible have the lights changed, or simply do not turn them on. Turn off computers when not in use as they can give out a high-pitched sound.

- The child may hear something very irritating and not be aware that others can't hear it and therefore will not think to tell the teacher that it is a problem. For example, he may hear the tap dripping next door, but not ask for it to be turned off, because he thinks the teacher already knows it's dripping. In fact that goes for all the senses. The child may smell food from the canteen in the next school block, or be irritated by a crease in his sock and presume that everyone can smell the food, or has socks that crease. If the child seems distracted, rather than insisting that he sit up and listen, ask if there is anything bothering him. You may be surprised at what you learn.

- If a child suddenly displays unusual behaviours, consider what may have changed in the classroom or environment. For example, the child may have loved painting but when the class started sketching, he hates art. Perhaps this child does not like the sound of the pencil scratching on paper. Perhaps a child liked running, but refused to run when the coach started using a whistle. Think of all senses, and ask why the child does the things he does.

- If a child says that something is too loud, or hurts his ears, or clutches his ears, then take him seriously. No child does that sort of thing for fun. Something hurts and the child cannot control the environment, but you can.

- Noisy places can be very upsetting and disturbing for the child, such as school assemblies, gymnasiums, cafeterias, sports days with lots of cheering, outings to theatres and concerts. Prepare the child for what to expect. Let him use earphones, iPods, earplugs, if necessary. Allow the child to sit on the end of a row so that he has a bit more personal space. In extreme cases, it may be best if the child is allowed to miss this activity.

- If the child is able to control external noise to some degree, he is able to cope better. At a school concert, let the child control the music, or teach him how to set up the microphones, for example.

- Warn the child if there will be a fire drill that day. This knowledge, of course, may unsettle the child, as he may be tense until the alarm is over. If possible, give advance warning just minutes before the alarm. Help the child understand the importance of the noise. 'The fire alarm is very important because it warns people to get to safety if there is a fire.' It may not help ease the pain of the noise, but it may help  take the fear out of the sound. Explain how long the drill is likely to take and assure him that the day's schedule will resume after the drill.

- Providing deep pressure input across the legs or arms or on the back, or allowing vigorous exercise before entering a noisy place, can help the child to keep calm.

- A child with auditory sensitivities may have difficulties regulating his own noise levels. The child may use a loud voice in places where silence is expected, such as in a library or at assemblies. He may bang things or stomp loudly or crash books down in an exam or test. If this is the case with your student, then realize that the child is not trying to be disruptive and simply needs to be taught the correct sound levels for each situation. With the child, listen to sounds that others make and rate each sound out of 10. For example, stomping on stairs is a 7. Dropping a ruler is a 4. Yelling on a sports day is a 10. Whispering is a 2. Help the child grade his own sounds so he has an awareness of their levels. Then in a given situation state an acceptable noise level: 'You are now going into a library. No sounds louder than a 3 are allowed.'

Classroom activities

- Have the children rub their hands over their ears, while one person plays with the volume knob of the radio making it randomly loud and soft. If the child with auditory problems is in the room, allow that child to be in charge of the radio as he will cope much better if in charge of the volume. You could add other irritating sounds such as a cymbal clashing unexpectedly, or a sudden screech of a recorder. All the while, teach something very new, such as words from a foreign language, and see how much the children can learn. Talk about how they would feel if they now got into trouble for not knowing these new words, or they failed a test when everyone else did well. Ask how they would feel if they got into trouble for asking the teacher to repeat an instruction or their friends mocked them if they asked them for help.

- Have the class sit very still with eyes closed and then, at your command, write down every sound that they can hear. Consider traffic noise, motor noises (e.g. fan, a/c), other voices, water sounds, weather sounds (thunder, rain, wind), animals and birds, and so on. Discuss the different sounds.

Who got the most? Which sound was least/most heard by the students? Ask the children to imagine that if all those sounds were just as loud as each other, how would that affect their lives?

- Play a guess-the-sound game. Play a recording of common noises in the classroom, and the children have to guess what they are. The hypersensitive child will most likely do very well at this game and that will boost his confidence. The hyposensitive child will learn to listen more closely to sounds.

Home link

- Encourage the learning of an instrument to help awareness of sounds and volume.

- Advise caregivers that gentle background music may help a child concentrate while doing homework and may also help him to sleep better.

- Warn the child when going to a potentially noisy place. If going to a party, for example, explain how many people may be there and tell the child that the noise levels might be high. Warn the child not to make too much noise himself (level 6 noise only) and, when there, find a safe quiet place that the child can retreat to if necessary, such as a balcony or garden.

- Help the caregiver to be aware that noisy places can be painful, frightening places for a child with auditory sensitivities. Encourage the caregiver to be aware of the child's distress levels and provide earphones or earplugs or, if necessary, be prepared to take the child away from the noisy places. Distracting the child from the noise or giving stress or fidget toys can also help.

- Warn the child if something noisy is going to happen in the house, such as vacuuming or using a blender or lawn-mower. Let the child go somewhere else or let him cover his ears.

Sight

Description

Vision is more than being able to see. It is also about making sense of what is seen. It helps people understand size and shape and colour and contrast and space. It helps with balance and body awareness. Many children who have 20/20 vision can still have a lot of visual problems and they may be *hypersensitive* or *hyposensitive* to input. It is interesting to note that both hyper- and hyposensitivity can create similar difficulties from opposite problems. Also a child may fluctuate from hyper- to hyposensitivities in a single day depending on mood, temperature, tiredness, and so on, so be prepared to vary your responses to difficulties.

Hypersensitive means that the visual system is over-responsive and the child does not seek stimulation. The child:

- has excellent vision and sees things that others don't see

- may be exceptionally good at activities that require visual search abilities (e.g. finding Wally in *Where's Wally* books) and prefers to concentrate on fine details rather than the big picture

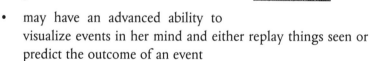

- may have an advanced ability to visualize events in her mind and either replay things seen or predict the outcome of an event

- enjoys playing in the dark or in dark places such as closets or closed-in areas

- will notice when things have been moved or changed

- may be overwhelmed with visual input and not be able to differentiate important details (school work written on the board) from unimportant details (a beetle walking across the board)

- may have difficulties copying work from a board or from books

- may complain that letters jump around on the page and pictures fragment into different parts

- may complain that her eyes have 'snow' in them or that she can see floaters in the eye

- may complain that still objects are moving or vibrating

- may complain of seeing after-images, or 'ghosts' of images, after looking away from a bright object

- may avoid bright places, and squint in the sun (especially when photos are being taken) and prefer to be in the shade; may hate being on the sunny side of a vehicle

- may be able to see the flickering of a fluorescent light and dislike strong artificial lighting, preferring dim or gentle lighting

- is distracted in a room with a lot of visual stimulations, such as things hanging from the ceilings

- can find messy rooms and messy desks stressful due to their clutter

- may dislike direct eye-contact and may prefer to look at objects rather than people

- can tire easily and may squint and rub her eyes or get headaches when having to do close visual work (e.g. reading, writing, computer work, drawing)

- may find strongly coloured or complex images hard to understand

- may prefer, or alternatively avoid, a certain colour and may even feel physically ill or great delight when looking at that colour; may prefer one coloured food over another or dislike a certain coloured toy

- may find it hard to track a ball or moving objects

- may look at objects out of the corner of her eyes, and/or tilt her head to see more clearly

- may be startled or frightened if things appear suddenly in her sight, especially if from a periphery

- is easily distracted by movement outside windows, on a screen, or out of the corner of her eyes; can see, and be distracted by, dust motes in the air, especially in streams of sunlight

- may hyper-fixate on one object and appear to stare at nothing with great intensity

- may flick fingers in front of her eyes, enjoying watching the movement; this also may occur if a child has poor body awareness so flicks fingers to create extra sensory input to tell her where she is in space.

- may get headaches and nausea from too much visual input and can experience sensory blackouts in situations of extreme input where she can lose sight for a short period of time

- may find visual input distracting when needing to concentrate on other senses; may stare at the floor or shut her eyes or refuse to look at a face when trying to listen, or alternatively may shut down other senses in order to concentrate on sight; may turn off music or TV when trying to read or may fail to hear verbal instructions while concentrating on written work.

Hyposensitive means that the visual system is under-responsive and the child craves stimulation. The child:

- may thrive on lots of visual input and love bright lights, contrasting colours, shiny surfaces, and may love watching spinning objects

- may miss visual clues and can't see what is in front of her

- may have trouble finding things, especially in a cluttered area; may see a specific object but have trouble seeing other objects around it

- may touch things to help her understand what she is seeing, especially in an unfamiliar place

- may have trouble reading and find it difficult to track the words across the page, and often loses her place

- does not see mistakes in her own work

- has trouble doing jigsaw puzzles, cutting in a straight line, tracing shapes; colours outside boundaries and generally has messy work; finds it hard to keep straight lines and to make letters an even shape; lines up maths problems poorly

- has trouble tracking moving objects and has poor hand–eye coordination

- may have difficulties following written instructions

- can mix up similar letters, p and q or d and b, and reverses similar words, for example saw and was

- has trouble telling different shapes and colours apart (e.g. square and rectangle, red and orange)

- can complain of seeing double

- may confuse left and right

- may have trouble with spatial awareness and may bump into objects and people (see **Balance: Vestibular System** and **Body Awareness: Proprioception**)

- may walk on toes as unsure where to place feet as she walks

- prefers to look out of the corner of her eyes and says that the middle is blurry but the edges are sharp.

HOW YOUR STUDENT MAY EXPLAIN IT

- Bright lights, flickering lights, headlights at night and especially sunlight is very painful for me. It's like the light is a physical thing trying to hurt me. Rather than just shielding my eyes, I try to push the light away with my hands.

- I always wear a cap as it not only shields my eyes from the sun or from above lighting; I can also pull it down further and further to reduce my field of vision so there are fewer things to distract me.

- I see things others don't see. Have you ever noticed dust motes in a stream of sunlight or the pattern of light on a wall? Well, I see them everywhere. I see the flash of light on ice skates; the multicolour colour of a beetle's back. Sometimes these things are nice to look at, but at other times, especially if I see them out of the corner of my eye, can cause severe physical pain like my head wants to explode.

- People just don't understand that if I am forced to look at their face when they speak, I cannot concentrate on what they are saying. I get too distracted by creases of skin and movements of lips and hair. I can hear much better when I look at the floor. But then I get yelled at for not being polite. I can't win.

At school

First of all, if you suspect that your student has visual problems, then make sure she has a basic eye test. It may simply mean that the child needs glasses. However, often a child with visual issues can have 20/20 vision. If this is the case then take the time to learn your student's visual needs. A hypersensitive child will need very different help and classroom set-up from a hyposensitive child.

Here are some ways you can help a child with visual issues:

- Generally, a structured, uncluttered classroom promotes the best learning environment for a child with visual issues.

- Be aware how hard a child with sensory issues has to work and give frequent breaks.

- Teach the child organizational techniques, such as labelling books or sections in books for different subjects. Only put out the books/equipment needed for the subject being taught at that time.

- Be aware of the other senses when the child struggles with visual issues. The child may read better, or worse, with music playing in the background. The child may have to try so hard with reading that she will not hear your instructions to stop work. If the child is over-stimulated with visual images (things hanging from ceilings, people walking past windows, shadows on walls) she might become over-sensitive to other sensations too, such as the smell of sweaty bodies in the classroom, or the sound of the dripping tap next door. This can all lead to restless, inattentive behaviours which may be misinterpreted as being naughty. Give your 'naughty' child the benefit of the doubt and ask if anything is wrong. If the child is unable to state any problems, think through the senses for yourself and see if you can make a connection. Give the child time to be by herself for a short while in a safety corner, or give her a job to do delivering a message to another classroom. Or give a toilet break and allow the child to go for a walk. Ignoring a child's discomfort could initiate a meltdown or, at the very least, considerable stress for the child.

- Seat the child at the front of the room where there are fewer distractions, and/or at the end of a row so she only has to deal with one person close by.

- Do not place a child where she is working in direct sunlight; however, filtered natural light is much better than overhead lighting.

- Allow, and even encourage, the child to wear a cap indoors as this alleviates glare/flicker from overhead lighting and can also help to minimize visual distractions if the cap is pulled low on the forehead.

- If possible, get fluorescent lights removed, or do not turn them on as the hypersensitive child can see them flickering. Also, the child with hearing hypersensitivity can hear them humming. If lighting is necessary, opt for a lamp with a light bulb.

- Encourage the child to wear sunglasses and hat outside to help with glare.

- If going on an excursion, be sure to sit the child on the shaded side of the vehicle and ensure that the child brings sunglasses and hat.

- Dim the computer screen or get a specialized screen to reduce glare. Change the screen background colour to one the child feels comfortable with (try off-white first), and when typing, increase the font size and experiment with styles to ease eye strain. Be sure to allow the child to take a break from screen time on a regular basis.

- If glare causes problems for the child, or if she is squinting while working, try putting black cardboard over the working space under the work books.

- If the child has trouble organizing maths problems neatly, encourage the use of grid paper.

- Some people with visual issues have found that tinted eyeglasses (such as Irlen spectral filters; see http://irlen.com) help a lot in reducing eye strain, glare and headaches. Be aware that not all specialists agree with this technique, so approach caregivers cautiously on this subject and respect their views. Alternatively, allow the child to wear mildly tinted sunglasses in class.

- Allow the child to track words with her finger when reading or use a marker to underline each line.

- Provide activities such as dot-to-dots, mazes and spot the difference puzzles to assist with tracking and observation skills.

- To help the child concentrate on her work without visual distractions, create a work space with high sides and no clutter.

- Experiment with using different-coloured papers when printing out class work. Often pastel-coloured paper is gentler on the eye. Let the child choose which colour suits best.

- If the child complains of letters and words jumping over the page, try putting coloured plastic over the page.

- If reading is a problem, try using a tilted desk, such as a drafting table, or raise the back of the book so the angle of reading is less than 45 degrees. This may also help with poor handwriting.

- Once you know that the child has your attention, do not insist that she looks at you when you are speaking. The hypersensitive child will actually listen and learn better if not overwhelmed with visual input, and the expressive, talking face has a lot of visual input!

- If printing out instructions or information, be sure to leave lots of breaks. A page full of writing is hard for the child with visual issues to take in.

- Avoid giving verbal-only instructions. Write instructions on the board, but avoid making the child copy them down as this is a major task all of its own. For long-term instructions, give hand-out sheets.

- Play bat and ball and hand–eye coordination games to develop tracking skills.

Creating a learning environment for visual learners

Many children with Asperger's are visual learners. Unfortunately, many teaching methods are not visual but rather are auditory, sequential, tactile and/or rote. The visual learners learn by seeing how things work, by placing this knowledge into context, and can also benefit from tactile learning such as physically manipulating objects. If a visual learner does not grasp a concept, forcing her to do extra rote learning will not help. However, once a visual learner does grasp a concept, then she will know exactly what to do. Forcing a visual learner to go through tedious steps to come to an answer (such as in mathematical sums) will be very frustrating for her.

Here are some ways you can create a learning environment for visual learners:

- Make sure the child knows the context of what is to be learned. Go over old work first, and mention what will come next. Give the big picture overview before teaching a new section.

- Use props: charts, graphs, maps, mind maps, photos, images, movies, hands-on materials, PowerPoints, and so on.

- Choose text and reading books that are illustrated with lots of pictures or diagrams.

- Relate the child's own experiences to what is to be taught.

- Avoid giving verbal-only instructions. Be sure to write instructions on a board or hand them out on paper.

- Have the children brainstorm for ideas rather than telling them what to do.

- Encourage creative ideas, even if they are wrong.

- Encourage the child to highlight important work in books and colour-code information.

- Get her to make lists of what is to be done, and cross off work as it is completed.

- Once you know that the child has your attention, allow the child to doodle while you speak. You may be surprised how much that can help a visual learner learn.

Classroom activities

Discuss how not all eyes work the same way and that even though people can look at the same things, they may see those things differently:

- Have the class look through a magnifying glass and discuss how the middle section is clear, but the edges are blurry. Explain how some children's eyes work like that and so it is hard for them to see things at the edge of their vision.

- Get the children to wear magnifying eyeglasses so what they see is blurry. Discuss how hard it would be to catch a ball, or write neatly, if they saw things like that all the time.

- Give the children a tube to look through, or roll up some paper to make a tube. Then ask them to copy some work from the board but they can only look through the tube while doing so. Discuss how they feel. Was this easy or hard? Enjoyable or frustrating?

Home link

- Discuss with the caregiver any visual concerns you have about the child. If necessary, suggest that the child has a vision test to confirm or eliminate the need for glasses. If the child's vision is fine then discuss the need for further assistance from an ophthalmologist or other specialists.

- Share with the caregiver the actions you take in the classroom to assist in reading and writing. Learn from the caregiver things that work at home.

- Keep a class diary that goes from caregiver to teacher daily so that both parties know what is happening and what is expected.

- Encourage the keeping of a journal for everything from school assignments to recording family trips. A child will remember better with this visual prompting.

- Make lists/timetables, charts/calendars at home for chores, events, and so on.

- Teach the child to keep her room tidy by providing set labelled places, for clothes, etc.

- When travelling, avoid seating the child on the sunny side of the vehicle and let the child wear sunglasses and a hat whenever they feel the glare is too much – even indoors.

- Avoid fluorescent lights in the house.

Smell

Description

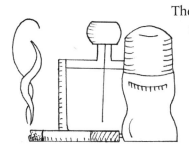

The sense of smell affects more than just the nose. It is intricately entwined with the sense of taste, and that is why your food seems bland when you have a cold. Smell is also linked closely to memories: a whiff of a long-forgotten odour can take you back to your childhood; a bad smell can remind you of a scary memory or a good smell can bring back feelings of being loved or happy. A child with sensory issues with smell can be *hypersensitive* or *hyposensitive*.

Hypersensitive means that the olfactory (smell) system is over-responsive and the child has a heightened sense of smell. The child:

- has a powerful sense of smell and can smell things other people cannot

- will be the first to notice smoke, fire, gas, fumes and other strong odours

- can smell odours a long way away and can smell lingering odours of things long gone, for example he knows that someone had smoked in a room a week earlier

- can tell if food is off by its smell, long before anyone else can

- is very aware of, and usually dislikes, any strong odours such as perfumes, deodorants, washing powder, cigarette smoke

- often tells people that they smell bad or good

- may refuse to eat food because of its smell and may hate a caregiver cooking certain foods

- may have the opposite reaction to common smells than other people; for example, may hate the smell of cookies, but love sniffing onions

- may get headaches and migraines and violent reactions from smells; even the slightest hint of some perfumes and solutions and items can cause instant headaches and vomiting

- may decide he likes/dislikes someone purely by his smell

- may avoid going into some shops and houses because of the scents there

- may love a certain scent and use it all the time and find comfort in smelling it

- can distinguish different foods and flavours in a mixed dish; for example, can tell the ingredients of a stew, or know the difference between various chocolate milk powders

- tends to prefer bland food without strong smells

- may have seasonal issues with pollen or moulds.

Hyposensitive means that the olfactory (smell) system is under-responsive and the child craves stimulation. The child:

- seems unaware of unpleasant odours, including his own body odour

- may eat food that is off as he can't smell that it is rotting or bad

- is in danger of drinking or eating poisonous things as he is not put off by the smell

- will be a safety risk as he is unlikely to notice smoke, fire, gas, fumes and other dangerous odours

- may lick things in order to get a sense of what it is, or bring objects close to his nose for deep sniffing

- may try to sniff another person when they meet

- complains that all food tastes the same

- may seek out strong smells, even those disgusting to others, such as faeces or a dirty diaper.

HOW YOUR STUDENT MAY EXPLAIN IT

💡 I hate the smell of my teacher's hair. When she leans over my desk to help me with my work, I want to puke. I get an instant headache and I can't remember anything she tells me.

💡 The smell of other people's body odour after sports activities is a nightmare for me. I get physical pain, headaches, body aches, nausea, and sometimes I even throw up. Then all my other senses go into hyperdrive too. I usually try to skip school on sporting days. It just hurts too much.

💡 Vanilla is my favourite scent ever. I absolutely love it. I wear it every day and eat anything with vanilla in it. I use vanilla soap and vanilla shampoo and burn vanilla candles. It calms me down and makes me happy. I feel better all over when I smell vanilla.

💡 People call me a bloodhound because I can smell even the tiniest hint of smoke. Cigarette smoke is the worst and makes my eyes water and my throat sore, even if the smoker is not smoking at the time. If I am in a shopping centre I can point to every person who smokes, even those a long way away from me. One day I might smell a real fire before anyone else does and save someone's life. That would be neat.

At school

It is important to consider that odours may be the cause of your child's anxiety, restlessness, 'naughtiness' or illnesses. School can be a very smelly place. Put thirty bodies into one room on a hot afternoon after sport and the smell is overpowering. Open tins of paint and use marker pens, and the fumes are toxic. As a teacher, if you wash your clothes in nice-smelling washing powder, wash your hair in sweet-smelling shampoo, clean your teeth with minty freshener and wear lovely perfume or aftershave to school, then you are a walking, talking cocktail of odours. You might think you smell great, but your hypersensitive student may reel in shock and even feel physically sick every time you walk past.

Here are some ways you can help children who are over-sensitive to odours:

- If you are concerned that your student has olfactory issues, then avoid wearing any strong-scented perfumes or deodorants while in class. If the child avoids getting close to you, try asking what is the matter. If it has something to do with how you smell, then most likely you will get an honest reply!

- There can be a multitude of reasons for a child to have headaches and feel nauseous; however, if you are aware that your student already has other sensory issues, then take into account what the child is smelling. Make a record of when the child complains of feeling sick. If it is consistently immediately after sport when the children are very sweaty, there might be your clue. It might be that the child is sick every art lesson. Another clue. Try letting the child sit outside, or by an open window, if odours in the room are strong. If the child avoids wearing his own clothes, for example won't put on a jacket when it is cold, perhaps the scent of his own washing powder is the culprit. It is a bit of trial-and-error, but if you can eliminate something as simple as an offending odour in the classroom then life will be better for all involved.

- Never force a child to endure smells that are making him unwell. Allow the child to go for a walk, or lie down in the sick room, or work in a more ventilated area.

- Canteens can be horrendous places for a hypersensitive child. The smells, the noise, the bright lights and the bustling bodies can become unbearable. Allow the child to bring his own lunch to school and eat outside, or in the classroom.

- Often a child will have at least one scent that is calming for him. Encourage the child to bring a handkerchief or cloth or small container that smells of something he likes and place it near his face when other smells overwhelm. If permitted, experiment with scented candles or incense sticks in the classroom. If you can find one your student likes, then it can help calm and focus the child. Often the more natural scents such as pine or mint are preferred to artificial ones.

- Teach and encourage good manners and tactful ways of expressing displeasure at a smell. Explain that it is not acceptable behaviour to tell a headteacher, for example, that his breath smells like rotten eggs. Teach a child when it is okay and not okay to comment on personal odours. Explain that to simply move away from a person with body odour is socially much more acceptable than saying out loud 'You smell.'

- For children who are hyposensitive, promote activities that use strong smells, such as playing with scented play-dough, cooking spicy foods, making scented candles.

Classroom activities

- Discuss and explore the importance of smell. Investigate how animals smell in a different way from humans and how a dog's sense of smell can be used to help humans. Consider the safety aspects of smell (e.g. warning of fire, bad food) and what would be the implications if you couldn't smell anything much, or could smell everything too much.

- Fill covered containers/jars with different-smelling items such as mint, crayons, pencil shavings, cookies, coffee, garlic, vanilla. The children have to sniff each one and try to guess what is inside. As a variation to this, have two of each container, and the children have to try to match up the pairs. Then discuss how easy/hard the children found this activity. What was their favourite/least favourite smell? Did any of the smells remind them of anything personal (vanilla might remind someone of Granny's cooking).

- Use the same covered containers with the different scents inside them and number them all. Bring a child to the front, blindfold him and ask him to pick a number. Then tell a story about the container that was chosen, but it does not have to be true (e.g. if giving garlic, say it smells like flowers). The child then tells how he felt, expecting one smell but getting another. Then when the next child comes up, tell a true story (e.g. if giving mint, say it is pleasant and fresh). This child will expect the opposite and get a surprise. Discuss how scary it would be if life was like that all the time – never knowing how something will smell and being afraid it will be horrible even if others say it is nice.

Home link

- Make caregivers aware of the different issues for hyper- and hyposensitivities. Suggest they keep a close watch for strong scents in the home that may aggravate/calm the child. It is best to use non-scented products wherever possible. Try using natural cleaning products in the home, such as bicarbonate of soda and vinegar.

- If a child does not like wearing certain clothes, it may be due to touch sensitivities, or to smell. Consider changing the washing powder, or airing the cupboard where the clothes are stored.

- If the child is unreasonably restless or unsettled, experiment with different-smelling washing liquids, shampoos, toothpastes, perfumes, candles, and so on.

- Help the child settle during homework time by having a scent close by that he likes. This can also help with memory recall later if the child takes that scent into the classroom.

- For younger children with smell and taste hyposensitivities, it is best to lock all cupboards containing poisonous items, such as bleaches, as the child may drink or eat these without the taste or smell deterring them.

Taste

Description

A child with taste and oral sensory issues finds some foods and drinks extremely distasteful or pleasurable and may either love or hate having non-food items in their mouth (e.g. a spoon or toothbrush).

As a regular classroom teacher, normally it is not your responsibility to feed a child or dictate a suitable diet. It is not your role to insist that a child eats her lunch or choose appropriate items from a canteen, unless this has been discussed carefully with the child's caregivers. However, regardless of your role, it is important that you are aware of what the child eats, or does not eat, as an undernourished, dehydrated and hungry child will perform badly in a classroom. Always remember that a child with genuine taste sensitivities is not trying to be difficult or different. She would like to eat what others eat; however, the taste of some foods can be slimy or foul or just plain wrong and the eating experience might be extremely stressful. Alternatively, there may be only one or two things she loves to eat and will ignore all other foods. This is a genuine problem and should be approached with understanding and encouragement rather than punishment and criticism.

On the plus side, when a child finds a food she loves, it can be an overwhelmingly lovely experience; the smell of the cookie, the crunch it makes when bitten into, the filling of taste buds with sweet cream can all combine to take away every other sense. A pleasurable taste experience can be used to calm a child, or reward positive behaviours. Remember, never give a child anything to eat without caregiver permission. A taste-sensitive child can be *hypersensitive* or *hyposensitive*.

Hypersensitive means that the taste buds are over-responsive and the child does not seek stimulation. The child:

- prefers bland foods and is very cautious of what she puts in her mouth

- can find some flavours unbearably bitter or spicy and yet happily eat others that seem similar; for example, may love lemons but hate grapefruit or may love black pepper but hate hot peppers

- dislikes foods touching on a plate and may eat food in a set order

- can be physically ill, such as gag or vomit, if forced to eat certain foods

- is predictable, can eat the same foods day after day and resists change to diet

- can be an extremely picky eater and eats a very small variety of foods; may hate eating out, even at friends' homes, and dislikes going to restaurants

- may be socially isolated when she won't eat what others eat

- may dislike mixed textures, such as soft toppings on crunchy pizza base, meat lumps in a casserole, burger meat in a bun

- dislikes certain textures and craves others; for example, might love mushy food but not crunchy food and prefer 'still' drinks to fizzy ones

- may enjoy food that is all the same colour on her plate; for example, on a 'white' day may only eat potato, cauliflower and chicken

- can taste miniscule flavours that others are oblivious to; may not like to drink from washed cups as the dishwashing liquid flavour can be tasted; if she hates a certain vegetable, such as mushrooms, forget about sneaking it into a meal as she will always know it is there

- may prefer food to be all the same temperature

- is afraid of choking and has difficulty with chewing and swallowing

- can limit herself to specific tastes, textures and colours of foods and this restrictive diet can be a health issue; in these cases it is recommended that a dietician or health specialist is consulted

- is very afraid of going to the dentist and hates having dental tools in her mouth

- doesn't like having teeth brushed and dislikes the taste of certain toothpastes and dental rinses

- hates licking stamps or stickers

- may hate non-food items in her mouth, such as cutlery and toothbrush

- may only drink from certain cups and use certain cutlery.

Hyposensitive means that the taste buds are under-responsive and the child craves stimulation. The child:

- may chew or lick or eat unsuitable objects such as clothes, furniture, pebbles, grass; this disorder is known as *pica*

- likes things in her mouth and chews nails, hair, fingers, pens, pencils

- likes foods with very strong tastes such as extra spicy, overly sweet or sour or salty

- states that many foods seem to taste the same

- enjoys brushing teeth, especially with a vibrating toothbrush

- actually enjoys going to the dentist

- enjoys foods with lots of texture; prefers crunchy foods and fizzy drinks.

HOW YOUR STUDENT MAY EXPLAIN IT

💡 I hate it when foods are mixed. I can't stand sandwiches with fillings or pizza with toppings. The different textures make me gag or want to vomit. Even the thought of eating a hot dog makes me ill. I get shivers even thinking about it!

💡 It's silly when people tell me food is good for me and therefore I should eat it. If something is slimy and smells like dog droppings would you put it in your mouth? If you force me to eat, then I will only throw it up again, so how can that be good for me?

💡 I love fizzy drinks. I could drink them all day just to get the tickly feeling in my throat. But I can always taste chemicals in water. No matter how clean the cup is, I can taste the dishwashing liquid, and it's icky to drink.

At school

- The smell of a school canteen or eating area may be horrendous and affect the taste of food. Also the noise in enclosed eating areas is notoriously loud. Allow the child to eat outside or in a place where the odours and sounds aren't so bad.

- Be aware that the child may have a lack of energy if not eating properly. If this is suspected, then talk to the caregivers about seeking professional help.

- Sometimes a child will mix up the sensory inputs she receives. A grumbling, hungry tummy could be confused with sound overload, for example, and so the child does not seek food, but rather puts her hands over the ears. A child may not understand the feeling of hunger and will not eat unless reminded to. For this reason, regular eating times are important, and a child must not be kept in class so that a lunch-eating time is missed, as seeing other children eat is a reminder for her to eat.

- Teach and encourage good manners and tactful ways of expressing displeasure at a taste. Explain that it is not acceptable behaviour to tell the lady at a school canteen, for example, that the sandwiches taste like puke. Teach a child when it is okay and not okay to comment on taste. Explain that to simply say 'No thanks' is socially much more acceptable than saying out loud 'Yuck, I hate that food.'

Hypersensitivity

- Often a child with sensory issues will refuse to drink at school, no matter how hot it is, or how much exercise the child has had. Obviously this may become a source of concern, especially in hot weather. Talk to the child to try to work out why she will not drink. Think of all the senses. Perhaps the school water smells different from the water at home. If so, bring water from home. Perhaps the child does not like the feel of the water canteen on her lips. Then let the child drink from a cup or a straw. Perhaps leaning over water taps is disorientating for a child with vestibular issues. Then let her bring her own water. Perhaps the child hates the taste of the chloride or fluoride put into the water. Or she can taste the detergent that the vessel was washed with. In this case allow the child to drink bottled water of choice, or flavoured water, or iced tea. The trick is experimenting and being flexible.

- Because a child with oral and taste sensitivities may also have touch hypersensitivities, she may settle better during eating time if she has a weighted blanket over her legs, or wears a weighted vest. Even wearing a tight-fitting cap can help her to eat better.

- Use nutritional facts and logic to encourage a child to eat. If a child understands that vitamin B12, for example, is essential to make her smarter, than she is more likely to be enticed to eat vitamin B12-rich food.

- Relate the body's need for food to a child's special interest; for example, 'Your body needs food like a steam train needs coal' or '…like a stegosaurus needed plants.'

- Let the child bring her own food to class parties or on school excursions or camps.

- Never punish a child for not eating her food, but rather give specific praise for what she did eat: 'Good job, you ate all your carrot sticks today.' Particularly, never make a child sit past the eating time to finish food. The child needs a time to relax and move at break times.

- In extreme cases, some children on the spectrum have eating sensitivities so strong that they physically *can't* eat. They may recognize that they are hungry and want to eat, but their body won't let them, gagging and vomiting if forced. In cases like these, it is pointless to think that they will eventually eat something if they are hungry enough. Specialist treatment must be sought.

Hyposensitivity

(See **Activities to suck, chew and blow** in **Body Awareness: Proprioception**.)

- Be aware that children with hyposensitivities may taste or eat unsuitable or even poisonous items.

- If a child craves oral stimulation, then allow school-appropriate and age-appropriate chewing items in class such as chew toys and chew necklaces, or direct the child to a more acceptable food item such as chewing gum, hard candy, lollipops or healthy food snacks such as popcorn. Naturally, parents or carers must be consulted first before giving a child any food. Many schools do not allow chewing gum; however, the benefits for children with sensory issues are proven to be great. Taste, touch, smell, hearing, vestibular and proprioceptive sensitivities all benefit from chewing gum.

- If the child is chewing or licking unsuitable objects, it is possible that she may be simply seeking a strong sensory input and, if that is the case, divert her attention or try giving a squeeze ball or popping bubble wrap or the like which will direct her away from an oral input.

- Allow the child to have a water bottle on the desk with a drinking straw.

- Play games such as blowing bubbles, using whistles, cotton-ball soccer with a straw.

- Encourage the child to eat chewy and crunchy food at lunch-time, such as carrots, apples, pretzels, popcorn, crackers.

Classroom activities

- Show pictures of very unusual foods eaten in different countries, for example frogs' legs, snails, spiders, monkey brains. Get children to imagine being offered this food. How would they feel? Would they be prepared to have a taste? Could they eat a whole plate of it? What do they think the food would smell like? How would they feel if they were punished for not eating it? What would they do if there was a serious consequence for not eating the food? Would someone saying 'It's good for you' or 'What's wrong with you, everyone else eats it' help them eat it?

- Gather a collection of small things to taste, for example tiny pieces of fruit/vegetable/olive/pickle/gherkin, a few grains of sugar, a grain of coffee, a spoonful of jelly/custard/honey. Have them all hidden and all numbered. Bring a child to the front, blindfold her and ask her to pick a number. Then tell a story about the food that was chosen, but it does not have to be true (e.g. if giving lemon say how sweet it is, or if giving sugar, say that it tastes sour). Let the child eat the sample and then tell how she felt, expecting one thing but getting another. When the next child comes up, tell a true story (e.g. if giving something salty, then say it is salty). This child will expect the opposite and get a surprise. Discuss how scary it would be if life was like that all the time – never knowing how something will taste and being afraid it will be horrible even if it looks good.

Warning: Be careful of child allergies and never use nuts in this game, especially for younger children. Seek parental permission before giving a child any food.

- Encourage children to bring something they like best so that everyone else can have a small taste. Encourage your sensitive child to have tiny taste of other food. Be sure to get caregiver permission before giving any child any food.

Home link

Not eating or drinking a healthy diet at school does not automatically mean the child does not eat properly at home. There are many factors that can influence a child's eating habits in a school environment, such as the smells in the eating area, the weather, the proximity to other students and peer pressure not to eat the things the child likes. However, if you notice that the child is not eating properly then it is important that this be communicated to the parents and caregivers.

Suggestions you may give to caregivers of a child with eating / tasting issues

- If the child is not eating properly at home or at school then the child's general health should be assessed by a doctor. There are things other than taste sensitivities that can cause a child not to eat. Consider if the child feels pain when she eats. She may have gastrointestinal problems. Is the child on medication? Some medicines suppress appetites. Is the child depressed or anxious? This too can suppress appetites.

- Encourage the caregivers to keep a food diary where they list all the foods eaten and where, when and how they were eaten; for example, 'Four cracker biscuits at 5pm in front of the TV sitting with siblings.' If kept over a week or so, this can give a better picture of what is actually eaten and may give a pattern of when the child is happy to eat and when she isn't.

- Make caregivers aware of what is not eaten at school, but let them know that you will not force a child to eat her school lunch or punish the child for not doing so. Be prepared to work with caregivers. Both you and the caregivers should always praise a child for whatever she *does* eat.

- Let caregivers know that many children on the autistic spectrum, but not all, find that casein-free and gluten-free diets help enormously with stomach/gut problems, and assist the child to concentrate, reducing irritability and generally promoting a feeling of wellbeing. Suggest a visit to a dietician.

- For younger children with smell and taste hyposensitivities, it is best to lock all cupboards containing poisonous items, such as bleaches, as the child may drink or eat these without the taste or smell deterring them.

Things caregivers can do to help the child eat and try new foods

- Encourage small tastes or even sniffs of new things and offer foods of different textures and colours and flavours.

- Talk to the child to work out why she likes a certain food. For example, if she eats potato crisps because she likes the crunchy dry feel, then she may be enticed to eat healthier alternatives such as unsalted popcorn or dried banana or wholegrain rice cakes.

- Eat together as a family so the child sees meal-times as a normal, happy routine of the day. Try to eat at the same time each day and allow the child to sit in the same chair and if necessary eat from the same plate and use the same cups and utensils. Once an eating pattern is established then introduce a change in the routine slowly so the child can become flexible enough to eat in different circumstances.

- Have specific eating times and do not allow snacking on 'bad' food that will lessen the desire for good food, and then give 'treat' food only after healthy food is eaten.

- Take the child's own food to restaurants and family outings.

- Allow the child to help prepare food as that may encourage eating it.

- Pick your fights – is it really worth the argument if she wants to eat breakfast food at dinner?

- At home and for school lunches, keep foods separate and give several choices or textures, flavours and colours, so the child has control over what she eats.

- Make a game out of eating. Play a board game and if you throw a six, then you eat a piece of apple.

- Be aware of how you phrase a question. If you say 'Would you like fish and chips and salad', it is very easy for the child to simply say 'No.' Instead, say 'We are having fish and chips and salad. Would you like all three or just one or two of those?'

Dental visits

Visits to the dentist can be major issues for children with any sensory issues. There are so many new sights, sounds, smells, tastes, things to touch, and chairs that move. It can be overwhelming. It may be best that caregivers arrange their own dental visits out of school hours, or the caregivers are present at a school dentist visit.

Here are some ways to make the dental visit easier for the child:

- Take the child to the dentist a day or two before her scheduled appointment and let her see the room. Ask the dentist to explain what will happen and show the tools she will use. Let the child sit in the chair and show how it moves.

- Let the child eat something chewy before the session.

- On the day, let the child wear the heavy X-ray vest the whole time to give deep pressure input. Also wearing a tight hat can help, and allow the child to hold a stress toy.

- Ask the dentist to explain each step so that nothing is a surprise.

- If the dentist has to touch the child, ask her to do so firmly rather than use a light touch. Light touches can be startling and painful for child with sensory issues.

- If the child is light-sensitive, let her wear her own sunglasses, or glasses supplied by the dentist.

- If the child is sound-sensitive, suggest that the dentist play calming music in the room or let the child wear her earphones with an iPod playing calming music.

- If the child has vestibular issues, then the movement of the chair may be terrifying. Some dentists allow the caregiver to hold the child instead of the child sitting in the chair. Or the child can sit in a regular chair or even lie flat on the floor.

- Don't tell the child 'It won't hurt' or 'Be brave' as this tells the child that it *might* hurt and she is still expected to be brave. Keep to the facts: 'The dentist will look into your mouth to see how well your teeth are.' If the child already thinks that a dentist will hurt, then say 'If it does hurt, then tell the dentist, and he will stop.' Give the child a sense of control.

Touch

Description

Touch is one of the senses that affects all parts of the body, registering temperature, pain and pressure. A tactile-sensitive child can be *hypersensitive* (over-responsive) or *hyposensitive* (under-responsive). However, many children can have strange combinations of both, and their reactions may vary from day to day and situation to situation.

If a child has other sensory issues then his reactions may be caused by a completely different sensitivity than first suspected; for example, a child might hate hugging, not because of a tactile hypersensitivity, but rather because he hates the perfume the hugger is wearing. Also many of the traits of a child with tactile sensitivities are the same traits displayed by a child with *proprioceptive* (body awareness; see **Body Awareness: Proprioception**) and *vestibular* (balance; see **Balance: Vestibular System**) issues and *pain* (see **Pain**) and it is recommended that those sections be read together with this section.

Hypersensitivity to touch means that the tactile system is over-responsive and the child does not seek stimulation. The child:

- may hate tags and labels on clothes as they cause great discomfort

- prefers soft, well-worn clothes and will often wear underpants and socks inside out

- avoids tucking in clothes, and wearing ties and other restrictive clothing

- avoids boisterous activities and crowds as even slight bumps can be very painful or uncomfortable

- tries to keep a large personal space around him at all times

- may be very startled or over-react to light contact in socially unacceptable ways, for example yells at or punches someone who accidentally jostles him

- hates being tickled, and the touching of sensitive parts, such as underarms, can provoke violent responses; this is important to remember if the child is young enough to be picked up

- hates being grabbed or touched from behind

- dislikes messy or dirty activities and avoids touching unfamiliar things and will wash hands frequently if forced to participate

- avoids getting face and hair washed and hates getting hair and nails cut

- may hate having hair in a tight ponytail

- tends to use fingertips to hold things rather than the whole hand

- will avoid anyone who tries to touch him, for example visiting relatives who pinch cheeks and give big hugs; may even avoid hugs and kisses and touching from family members

- does not seek physical contact with others and may withdraw socially

- hates standing in lines or where other people may touch him

- dislikes rough bed sheets, especially if old and pilled, and prefers soft blankets

- may feel pain and great displeasure from raindrops or water in a shower or even strong wind on his skin

- may have a low pain threshold for minor injuries such as scrapes and scratches, insect bites and getting thorns (see **Pain**)

- may be very scared of the dentist and hates brushing teeth (see **Dental visits** in **Taste**)

- avoids foods with certain tastes and textures (see **Taste**)

- may refuse to walk barefoot, especially on grass

- may walk on tip-toe.

Hyposensitivity to touch means that the tactile system is under-responsive and the child craves stimulation. The child:

- may not be aware of things touching him and might not realize that he has food on his face, or mud on his feet

- may not be bothered by twisted or back-to-front clothes and can be a messy dresser with shirt half-tucked, one sock up and another down, shoes untied

- enjoys touching things with texture and is always rubbing things between his fingers or fidgeting with objects

- has difficulties with fine motor control and will avoid and have trouble with writing, cutting, tying shoelaces and ties, buttoning, eating with utensils, and so on

- enjoys the sensation of crashing into and bumping things

- enjoys messy tactile activities such as finger painting and pottery or walking in mud or sand

- may love light tickling and touching

- seeks hugs and likes to sit in laps and desires constant contact from others

- may bump people and other objects and not seem to be aware of it

- often is too rough when playing and may hurt others and pets unintentionally (see **Body Awareness: Proprioception**)

- can have a high pain threshold and is not bothered by scrapes and cuts, getting thorns and even breaking bones (see **Pain**)

- may lick or bite himself and others (see **Taste**)

- may brush hair or teeth too hard and scratch itches too vigorously

- may self-harm: bite, pinch, bang head and even cut himself

- may not be able to identify objects by just touching them, for example those things at the back of a drawer or the bottom of a school bag; needs to see things to find them

- may be insensitive to temperature and not feel cold when others are wearing heavy jackets, or may burn himself in the shower by having water too hot

- may be insensitive to his own sicknesses and can have a fever and not realize it.

HOW YOUR STUDENT MAY EXPLAIN IT

Hypersensitivity

💡 The tags in clothes and the creases in seams feel like broken glass scratching me and it drives me crazy. All I can think about is how uncomfortable I feel and I miss things the teacher says because I am trying to sit in a way that I hurt less. Sometimes when people bump me the pain is like biting into tin foil on a tooth filling, or hitting a funny bone.

Hyposensitivity

💡 I love touching things and rubbing things between my fingers and squishing them in my hands. I am not sure why, but it makes me calmer and helps me concentrate. The teacher tells me to stop fidgeting and listen, but I listen much better when I do fidget. I love to bump into things as the crash feeling is great. I always want some sort of pressure on me somewhere so I lean on people or want squeezy hugs, or I bite my nails or I bend paper clips. As long as some part of me is touching or rubbing or banging something, then I feel good.

At school

In general

- Be aware that a child with tactile issues may be unwilling to try new activities, such as a new sport, as he is afraid that it may hurt him (hypersensitive) or if the sense of touch is underdeveloped (hyposensitive) then he will not have the fine or gross motor skills to perform it well. Never berate a child for his inabilities and do not foster an environment where other children can make fun of or bully the child with difficulties. Rather, encourage and support whenever needed.

- Consider that the child with tactile issues is often messy when it comes to art work and writing and general organization. Do not presume that the child knows what to do but just will not do it. The messiness is not due to laziness or carelessness but is often a genuine inability to physically perform the required task (write neatly between lines, wash brushes properly) or sense when he has dripped paint or spilt things. Instead of berating a child, give assistance and guidelines on how to order things, replace things, clean up messes, and so on.

- If the child bites himself and others (or cuts or otherwise self-harms) then this must be taken seriously. Keep a close record of every time a child bites and ask that the caregivers do the same. Watch for patterns. Perhaps the child bites close to meal-times and is expressing hunger. Perhaps it is when pushed or startled, showing a vestibular or touch issue. Perhaps the child is purely seeking strong sensory input. Only once the root cause is worked out can the biting be addressed properly. Often a specialist will need to be consulted.

Hypersensitivity

- Never touch a hypersensitive child without warning him first. Do not tap his shoulder or ruffle his hair or pat his back like you would to other students, even in a kind, friendly way. Light touches hurt and unexpected touches can be startling and even frightening.

- Teach the child safety sentences: 'Please don't touch me', 'I don't like it when you do that', 'Please stop.' Use colloquialisms suitable for his age.

- Always approach a child from the front so he is not startled by an accidental bump.

- In class, place the child's desk at the end of a row, or even on its own, so that he will not be accidentally touched so easily. Ensure that the child knows that an isolated desk is not a punishment, but rather an acknowledgement of a need. Naturally, if the child is upset at being 'isolated' then bring him back into the group.

- When the class is sitting on the floor, make sure the child is at the periphery and not in the centre of the group so that he is less jostled. Proximity to others on every side can be quite distressing.

- Let the child sit on a cushion as the hardness of the floor, or the prickliness of the carpet, can be unbearable.

- Allow students to cut off tags from clothing (with parental permission, of course).

- If permitted, allow the child to remove shoes in class if socks are rubbing or shoes hurting.

- Beware of the weather as the feel of the wind and rain can be extremely uncomfortable. Allow the child to remove wet clothes if he expresses discomfort.

- Allow the child to wear a hat, as appropriate and as desired. Alternatively, allow the child to not wear a hat if it causes discomfort.

- Let the child wear gloves, if desired, for messy tasks such as cleaning things or finger painting.

Hyposensitivity

- If the child is chewing things such as collars, sleeves, pencils and hair, or biting fingers and nails or other inappropriate objects, then provide oral stimulation activities to stimulate the tactile senses in the neck, jaw and head. (See **Activities to suck, chew and blow** in **Body Awareness: Proprioception**.)

- The child may find it easier to write with a hair tie around the wrist, then twisted around a pencil. This provides extra awareness of pencil pressure.

- The child may have problems with handwriting and can find it difficult to hold a pencil or pen. Allow the child to use pencils rather than pens even in later years. Use fatter pencils rather than thin ones. Supply a variety of pencil grips. Sometimes vibrating pens can help. Allow the child to print rather than forcing him to use script. And where and when feasible allow the use of computers for writing activities.

- Allow the child to have fidget toys in class, such as stress balls, squeezy toys, straws, bubble wrap (if the popping sound is not a problem), paper clips, pencils, and so on. Let him doodle. Most likely the child will be able to concentrate much better if he is doing something with his hands.

- Often a child will perform better if he wears a weighted vest or has a weighted blanket over his lap, or anything that gives a deep touch. Even wearing a backpack can help. Tie heavy door 'snakes' (the ones to keep out the draught) to the edge of chairs to wrap around the child when he sits down. Or make chair 'arms' out of old jeans' legs filled with beans, to give the child a chair hug.

- Be aware that the hyposensitive child often learns best while doing something, so incorporate activities into teaching a lesson; for example, cut up fruit when teaching fractions.

- Provide sensory activities for free time, or when the child is getting stressed, such as popping bubble wrap, jumping on a mini-trampoline, or running fingers through sand, rice or beans.

- In art time, finger-paint or paint with shaving cream; use putty or clay or play-dough.

- The hyposensitive child will perform better if allowed heavy muscle activities (see **Activities where the child has to push and pull** in **Body Awareness: Proprioception.**)

Classroom activities

- Have the children put a piece of sandpaper next to their skin in a place where it will rub, for example under the collar next to the neck, where the sock rubs against the shoe, in the armpit. Then sit on a hardcover book or piece of wood so that the edge is pressed against the skin. See how long they last before they start to complain, or they move the objects to a more comfortable position. Talk about how frustrating it is and how hard it is to concentrate when they are distracted.

- Create a Touchy-Feely bag full of items with different textures. The children have to reach in, hold one object and say what it is before drawing it out.

Home link

- Inform caregivers if uncomfortable clothing is an issue at school and work together, within school rules, to accommodate the child's needs. Perhaps allow the child to wear sports clothes all day as they are generally softer and more comfortable than formal uniforms. Cut off all tags and labels. If necessary, replace metal zips with buttons, or vice versa. Buy uniforms second-hand as they are already worn in. Wearing underwear and socks inside out can help. Sew a button inside the pocket of a child who needs to fidget, or line the pocket with silk or fur to give tactile input. Some girls may prefer leggings under dresses or sport clothes. Boys may prefer long trousers all year round, or shorts all year round. Be aware that some fabrics can be very scratchy and uncomfortable or may feel slimy to the child. Where possible, allow the child to choose his own clothes to buy and wear. Be as flexible as possible.

- A hypersensitive child is best grooming himself as he knows his own comfort boundaries. Let the child wash and brush his own hair and teeth, towel himself dry and, when old enough, cut fingernails.

- The hyposensitive child may enjoy a deep massage or very strong hug to help him to relax.

- A pet is a wonderful thing as the fur can be lovely to touch, the weight when it sits in a lap can calm a child, and its warmth and proximity are great to snuggle against.

- A hyposensitive child may like oral stimulation that is not necessarily anything to do with taste or hunger but be about the feel or touch of things in his mouth. In this case provide food that crunches or snaps, such as apples, carrots, pretzels, crackers or popcorn, or give foods with strong flavours such as dried fruit, sour candy, pickles, spices, curries.

- A hyposensitive child may love messy water play. Let him wash dishes or the car or the dog, play in mud, water the garden, walk in the rain and stomp in puddles. Give him a water pistol and let him loose!

- Some children find certain bed sheets very uncomfortable, especially ones with texture or ones that are pilled. They are more likely to prefer cotton sheets to flannelette ones.

- Encourage activities where touching occurs, such as martial arts, or ballet or acting, and be very supportive until the child is relaxed at a casual touch.

Balance

Vestibular System

Description

Apart from the five senses normally recognized – touch, taste, hearing, sight, smell – children with sensory issues may also have issues with balance (vestibular system) and body awareness (proprioception). The vestibular system, which is situated in the inner ear, helps people with balance and posture, and gives an understanding of how fast the body is moving. If the vestibular system is over-responsive, the child experiences *hypersensitivity* to balance and she does not seek stimulating movements. If the vestibular system is under-responsive then the child will experience *hyposensitivity* to balance and she will seek stimulating movements.

But nothing is ever simple with sensory disorders and some children will have a strange mix of hyper- and hypovestibular sensitivities. Also, some children will seek the very thing that makes them uncomfortable. They can't explain it, but just know that even though they don't like a sensation, they still want it. So even if a child does one of the activities on one list, it does not mean that the other issues on that list necessarily apply to her. There is also a strong overlap of symptoms with body awareness (proprioceptive) issues and, indeed, with all the senses. So when trying to address an issue, be flexible with your approach and try a variety of activities to help the child. A child who has problems with her vestibular system may be *hypersensitive* or *hyposensitive* to balance.

Hypersensitive means that the balance system is over-responsive so the child does not seek extra input. The child:

- may be afraid of ordinary movements (playground equipment such as slides or swings)

- may tolerate movement in one direction, for example up/ down, but hate movement in a different direction, for example sideways

- finds it difficult to walk on uneven surfaces and stairs

- dislikes elevators and escalators and may even sit down while they are moving

- gets motion sickness easily in cars, boats and planes

- may experience vertigo, even if the drop is just the height of a footpath to the road

- has an abnormal fear of her feet not being on the ground

- hates being upside down

- prefers quiet activities, and moves slowly and cautiously

- avoids risk-taking

- may cling to an adult or friend when there is no real need

- gets startled easily if bumped or her chair is pushed

- may find it hard to ride a bike or hop on one foot

- loses balance easily and will avoid situations where balance is required

- is clumsy and often bumps into things.

Hyposensitive means that the balance system is under-responsive so the child seeks extra input. The child:

- loves swings and slides and the scary rides at amusement centres

- enjoys spinning and running round in circles, the faster the better, and does not get dizzy

- loves crashing into things to get maximum input

- may walk with a strange gait or be a tip-toe walker

- can't sit still; is always moving, rocks backwards and forwards, shakes her body or legs or head while sitting

- loves to jump on trampolines, beds and furniture; spins in swivel chairs

- loves getting into upside-down positions or being tossed in the air

- loves sudden movements such as going over bumps on a bike or in a car

- has a dangerous sense of adventure

- has a great sense of balance and can reorientate herself quickly if falling (such as in skating or tripping over).

HOW YOUR STUDENT MAY EXPLAIN IT
Hypersensitivity

    ☼ I have terrible balance and I am always dropping, spilling and breaking things. I bump into people and things all the time, even when I try hard not to and I have so many bruises but mostly have no idea how I got them. I hate it when someone bumps my chair or kicks the back of it, because it startles me and I feel like I am falling. If someone grabs me when I don't expect it, it's such a scary thing that I will hit out at them before I can think. I feel seasick going down stairs and standing on the edge of even tiny drops. I never go on fairground rides, not even the 'baby' ones like the merry-go-round. Even watching the spinning ones makes me sick. Spinning things are like black holes that suck in my brain. My mind has to work so hard to understand what I am seeing, and then when I look away, I think the whole world is spinning.

Hyposensitivity

    ☼ I love spinning. The best thing ever is to go on the fastest rides at the fairground where I could spin for hours and never get dizzy. I love to crash into things and bang things because it makes my body feel alive. People are always telling me to 'calm down' or 'go slower' or 'stop running' but if I stay still then I feel so uncomfortable. I can't really explain it. It's not like I am in pain, but it's only when I am moving that I feel like I have proper balance; that I feel like I am me.

At school

It is important to find every reason to praise a child with Asperger Syndrome and to build her up in the eyes of her peers. If a child has hyposensitivities then she could have exceptionally good balance and would be able to reorientate quickly if she was about to fall, for example slipping on ice or when skating. The child might also be able to climb the highest or is the best diver because of lack of fear of heights. Praise these things specifically. Play spinning games, where she will excel, or let her talk about the huge, scary rollercoasters and theme park rides she enjoys so much. The other children will respect her 'bravery'.

The hypersensitive child will be extremely cautious about how she moves and may appear 'wimpy' to others. Praise the child when caution is necessary: 'Look how Jenny holds the rail when she comes down the stairs', 'Jack is always polite and never pushes or bumps anyone.'

Here are some ways you can help your child who has balance issues.

In general

- Some children with hyposensitivities to balance have been known to enjoy jumping from great heights, which is an obvious concern in a school situation. Yet those with hypersensitivities find heights scary and have difficulties with stairs and escalators. Be very aware of both extremes.

- In your classroom, alternate activities where the child must be still, with 'exercise time'. After twenty minutes or so, get the class up to do star jumps or jogging on the spot.

- Balance and body awareness issues combine to make many common school activities very difficult, such as catching a ball, jumping, hopping, skipping, dancing and sports that require good hand–eye coordination. However, all these skills are very important to develop, so modify lesson plans to accommodate the skill levels of your student. Never embarrass a child by pointing out her lack of skills, especially in front of peers. And never let peers criticize the child. Always praise specific improvements: 'Well done, you caught the ball three times in a row!'

- Play some fun 'sports' such as balloon volleyball and blowing and popping bubbles, which encourage hand–eye coordination and visual tracking skills. (*Beware:* some children with audio issues will hate any activities with balloons as the sound of a balloon popping is very frightening to them.)

- The child with balance problems often finds it hard to walk in a straight line, such as along corridors or even through rows of chairs. Teach her to gently touch the wall or the desk with the tips of fingers as she walks. Encourage holding on to handrails as she walks down stairs.

- Vestibular issues can also affect vision, as stationary objects may appear to be moving. Letters on the page can be blurry, or jump around, which naturally makes reading difficult. If possible, get large-print books or audio books for the child to read. Podcast and YouTube videos on relevant subject areas can help the child learn without having to do copious reading.

- If the child uses a computer in class, allow her to increase the font size when working on documents. Make sure she is placed so that glare is minimal and there are no distractions around the computer.

- A child with vestibular issues will most likely have issues with other sensory inputs as well. As you could imagine, she will be exhausted by the end of the day. The child may also be anxious and depressed. It is easily understood how it would be hard to memorize things and to focus for long periods of time with so many other things to contend with. Make your classroom a safe place. Be sensitive to how hard the child is working to simply be part of the class. Making allowances for the child to rest in a quiet corner, or alternatively bounce on a mini-trampoline for a few minutes, is recognizing a need, not showing preferential treatment to a spoiled child.

Hypersensitivity

- If a child hates movement, then be sensitive to this and introduce moving activities slowly.

- A child with vestibular hypersensitivity has low tolerance for movement as it makes her feel dizzy and nauseous and uncomfortable. She will have problems changing speed and direction. Sports where the participant must stop and start quickly, such as basketball or football, are a real problem for her. Be sensitive to these difficulties and place a child so that she can moderate and reduce her own movement. Perhaps the child could be the scorer for the day. Put yourself in the child's position. If you had a head cold and felt dizzy because your ears were blocked, would you want to have your peers yell at you because you dropped the ball?

- If it is age-appropriate and permitted in your school, hold the hypersensitive child's hand as you walk, especially up and down stairs. This is even more important on an excursion where the child is unfamiliar with the walking surface. Or, alternatively, get the children to hold hands as they walk.

- A hypersensitive child may react badly if she is suddenly moved, bumped or pushed. Her balance goes crazy and it can be a very disturbing experience for her. In the classroom, place the child's desk away from walkways so other children are unlikely to bump the chair. When lining up, place the child at the front or end of the lines where she is less likely to be hassled by other students.

At break times or at the end of the day, allow her to leave the classroom first or let her hang back until the bustling crowds ease.

- The hypersensitive child is already overloaded with input. Break down instructions and activities into small steps as she has to concentrate so hard to follow that often she will get left behind.

Hyposensitivity

- Make sure the child who seeks sensory input is given time on playground equipment that she especially enjoys, such as swings and slides. This could also become a lesson in taking turns, as once she gets on, she may not want to get off. Incorporate such activities into sports sessions.

Classroom activities

- To help others understand what it is like to have a vestibular problem, have children stand on an uneven surface, such as a board on top of a golf ball, or balance on a beam on the floor while standing on one leg or on their heels. Then have them try to catch a bean bag or ball without them unbalancing.

- Have the children spin around five times on the spot, then immediately throw them a ball. Or hold a broom or stick above their heads. Spin around three times looking at the broom. Then put the broom on the ground and try to jump over it. The children will soon realize how hard it is to catch anything or jump over things when they are feeling dizzy or unbalanced.

Home link

- Encourage caregivers to pursue the child's physical activities outside of the school to build up hand–eye coordination and confidence.

- Inform the caregivers that the child may have difficulties walking around in the dark as she may get very disorientated. Perhaps provide a night light so the child can get up safely at night if she has to.

- Discuss with the child's caregiver any issues or situations that occur at school; and if difficulties are beyond your time and ability to remedy, then suggest occupational therapy or other professional help.

- Let parents know that if a child is hypersensitive then she may have problems with motion sickness in cars, buses, planes and boats, or hate having her hair washed over a sink.

- A hammock or an enclosed cocoon-like swing can provide a safe cosy place with enjoyable motion. The hypersensitive child may resist this at first, but it is a fun and gentle way to encourage her to build up tolerance to movement.

Body Awareness

Proprioception

Description

Apart from the five senses normally recognized – touch, taste, hearing, sight, smell – children with Asperger Syndrome also may have issues with balance (vestibular system) and body awareness (proprioception).

Proprioception is the body giving information to the brain about where different body parts are, how they are moving, and how much pressure to apply in various situations. Right now, as you read this, you probably know that your feet are on the floor, or that your legs are crossed. You hold the page with the right amount of pressure so you don't tear the paper. You can reach for your coffee cup without bumping it off the table and bring it to your mouth without spilling a drop. A student with proprioceptive issues could have a problem with some or all of those actions you take for granted:

- Most commonly, people with proprioceptive issues are *hyposensitive,* meaning that their system is under-responsive to their body's position in space. They may slump or slouch and they will seek movements and activities to stimulate their body awareness.

- Less commonly, if the proprioceptive system is over-responsive, then people are *hypersensitive* to their position in space and they do not seek movements to stimulate their body awareness. They may appear rigid and tense.

- Most children with proprioceptive issues also have *low muscle tone* and *poor motor control.*

But nothing is ever simple with sensory disorders and some children will have a strange mix of sensitivities. The time of the day, their moods, their health and other events in their lives will affect their proprioceptive reactions.

The child with *hypersensitive* proprioceptive issues:

- resists tasks where he has to push and pull

- has stiff movements, locks joints, sits rigidly

- may need to turn the whole body to look at things

- prefers sedentary activities.

The child with *hyposensitive* proprioceptive issues:

- has poor depth perception

- may rock back and forth, or flap hands or stim in other ways so he can get a sense of where his body is in space

- loves pressure from weighted blankets or clothes

- enjoys the pressure of being 'squished' and will pull heavy things over himself and squeeze into tight places

- likes to bump, jump, stomp, push, crash, bang, shake, run, fall on the floor on purpose – anything to get stimulated – and often stimulates everyone else around him

- loves jumping on trampolines or off furniture

- when sitting, will tap fingers, shake legs, bang feet on ground

- likes to chew pens, fingers, hair, clothes, sleeves – anything, really

- bites nails, cracks knuckles, twirls hair, may self-bite and in extreme cases cut himself

- prefers tight clothes, such as leggings, turtle necks, hats, belts, hoods. Likes to have shoes done up very tightly or prefers heavy shoes or boots so he feels in control of his feet

- loves rough games, such as wrestling and tackling, and will give extra-strong bear hugs

- plays too rough; hits, bumps or pushes other children; can hurt them and himself

- does everything with a lot of force, for example slams doors, bangs objects down

- is noisy with toys – bangs and crashes them

- grinds his teeth in the day and/or while sleeping.

Low muscle tone and poor motor control
The child:

- has a floppy body and will sit slumped in chairs or at a desk, or flop against walls and other people

- may be clumsy, bump into other people

- finds it hard to do up buttons and tie shoelaces and ties

- has difficulty turning doorknobs and handles, opening and closing items

- finds it hard to stop himself from falling

- has poor gross motor skills: jumping, catching a ball, climbing a ladder, and so on

- has poor fine motor skills: difficulty using pencils, cutlery, scissors, and so on

- may be ambidextrous, switching hands for colouring, cutting, writing, and so on

- believe it or not, may have trouble licking an ice-cream!

- gets very tired easily

- misjudges the pressure needed for activities:
  - may break pencil tips by pressing too hard, or work is too faint to read
  - rips paper when erasing work

- ° often breaks toys and objects
- ° drops things easily or compensates by holding things too tightly
- ° may pet animals, or play with peers, too hard, hurting them.

HOW YOUR STUDENT MAY EXPLAIN IT

💡 If I have to sit for long in one place, I feel so uncomfortable, like I get lost in space. I don't know where my body is, so I have to move it. Then I am okay for a few minutes until the tension builds up and I have to move again. I never know where to put my arms or legs and so I like to squish them against something, like the edge of a table, or around the legs of a chair, or I lean on a wall, or I squeeze under something heavy, put my elbows on the table and lean my chin on my hands, or I cross my hands behind my head. All these things help me to know exactly where my body parts are. If I am forced to sit still, then I at least move my fingers. I rub my fingers along sharp edges of anything, a desk, a chair. I fiddle with my clothes, twist my hair, tap my fingers, bite my nails. If I don't do all that, it's like I don't exist.

💡 I am always getting into trouble for things I don't mean to do. I am often told I am too rough, and I hurt my friends and don't know what I did. I am always picked last for a sports team because I drop the ball and trip over when I run. I never know how hard to hold things and I break things all the time without meaning to. I am so clumsy and I often spill things and knock things over. Even when I see things in my way, and try to avoid them, my body doesn't obey and I bump into them anyway. I have lots of bruises and mostly I don't know where I got most of them. People say I am like a bull in a china shop, which is pretty silly, because a bull wouldn't even fit through the door of most china shops.

At school

In essence, a child with body awareness issues acts in a way to balance the input he is getting. He may appear disruptive, inattentive and even naughty. However, all that he doing is trying to calm or stimulate his body and make sense of the world. Understanding why your student behaves the way he does and providing appropriate activities and adjustments will make the world of difference to the child and to your classroom.

In general

- If a child has difficulties understanding his body's position in space, then he will also have difficulties understanding 'spatial' instructions. Instructions such as, 'Sit up straight' or 'Look to the front', or 'Write your name on the left' or 'Move backwards' can be very confusing. Even if the child understands the words and meaning behind the instructions, his body may not be so quick to obey. Be very aware that the child who seems to disobey your instructions may simply need a little more time to absorb what you have said, especially if you gave more than one instruction. Remember that many children with Asperger's are visual learners, so include visual aids with instructions, such as pointing to the left side of a page, or point to show the direction you want the child to go in, or write your instructions on the board.

- Just as a classroom for the blind must be laid out in a way that allows for maximum movement without harm to the child, likewise arrange your class so that those who are 'body blind' can move freely without fear of sharp edges, things jutting into walkways and shelves with things that could fall off when bumped.

- Outline the walkways and sitting areas with masking tape so that they are clear and obvious.

- When walking the class from one activity to the next, take the longest route to give the most exercise. Make a game of it. Get children to map different ways to navigate the school grounds.

- Balance and body awareness issues combine to make many common school activities very difficult, such as catching a ball, jumping, hopping, skipping, and sports that require good hand–eye coordination. Beware of this and adjust your lessons accordingly. Never embarrass your students by commenting negatively on their inabilities in this area.

- Be aware that doing up buttons and tying shoelaces and ties can be very difficult. Allow extra time for the child to change into, and out of, sports clothes or swimwear.

- A child may not be aware of how hard he is hitting or pushing something. He may hurt a peer by giving a friendly pat on the back or a high five that is overly forceful. Or he may kick a ball too hard or too softly and annoy peers. He may squeeze juice boxes too hard, spilling drink over himself and others. He may grasp things too softly and drop them. Or he may hold things too hard and break them. Always be aware that a child who appears too rough and unruly may have genuine body awareness issues and needs to be helped and not punished.

- Limit the number of items a child is asked to carry (such as carrying books and a guitar while wearing a backpack), as juggling many things is very difficult.

- Handwriting can often be an issue as those with weak muscle strength can find it hard to hold a pencil. Allow the child to use pencils rather than pens even in later years. Use fatter pencils rather than thin ones. Supply a variety of pencil grips. Sometimes vibrating pens can help. Allow the child to print rather than forcing him to use script. And where and when feasible allow the use of computers for writing activities.

Hypersensitivity

- Hypersensitive proprioception can cause a child to have to concentrate more and physically work harder than his peers, causing chronic fatigue. Give opportunities for the child to rest when needed. In sports, he could be the official scorer instead of the next batsman. During clean-up time, let the child wipe the board (gross motor) instead of picking up the tiny pieces of paper left over from art class (fine motor). If offering free-time activities to the class, make sure that at least one option is simply to rest.

- Allow the child to sit at the end of rows, or even at a desk on his own so that he has more space around him. Ensure that the child knows that an isolated desk is not a punishment, but rather an acknowledgement of a need. Naturally, if the child is upset at being 'isolated' then bring him back into the group.

- When the class is sitting on the floor, make sure the child is not in the centre of the group. Proximity to others on every side can be quite distressing. Allow the child to sit on a pillow which will delineate his own space.

- When walking with the class in lines, allow the child to be at the front or at the back, so that only one other person is near. Adopt a class rule that you walk one arm's length away from the person in front of you.

Hyposensitivity

- Hyposensitive proprioception can cause a child to feel extremely uncomfortable if forced to sit still for too long. Give opportunities for the child to be active when necessary. Send him on errands. Ask him to wipe the board or desks or empty the bins. If offering free-time activities to the class, make sure that at least one option is jump on a mini-trampoline or go for a run.

- In situations where a child *must* sit for long periods of time – such as in school assemblies, or watching a movie or school plays, allow him to take fidget toys, such as stress balls. If this is frowned on in your school then make these small enough to keep in a pocket so they do not distract others. Allow 'toilet' breaks which really means that the child can get out of the classroom and move for a little while. Make sure the child is at the end of rows so he only has to deal with a person on one side.

- When at his desk, allow the child to sit on sensory cushions or an exercise ball or swivel chair.

- If possible, provide a high table, the type that people may stand around at a party, so that the child can stand to work at will. Alternatively, allow the child to lie on his tummy on the floor to work. Lying a weighted blanket, or bean bag, over his back can settle him even more.

- Place a hair tie around the wrist and twist it around a pencil. This provides extra awareness of pencil pressure.

- Use a weighted vest or a weighted blanket in his lap when he sits at a desk.

- *Never* punish a hyposensitive child by taking away his play time or sports activities. The child needs to move and, if you prevent this, then problems will escalate.

Activities where the child has to push and pull

These build up muscle and joint strength and give sensory input to promote body awareness. If the child is experiencing major difficulties with muscle strength, it is best to do activities which do not require team work until the child's strength is built up so he can monitor his own effort and will not be embarrassed if he is the weakest one in a group.

The child can:

- lie on his tummy on roller boards and push himself along with arms

- do wall push-ups, normal push-ups, chair push-ups, pull-ups on a bar

- climb ropes and cargo nets, rock walls, ladders, and use climbing equipment in the playground and the gym

- sit back-to-back with another child, link arms and try to stand; or face each other, hold hands and try to stand by leaning out

- roll a weighted ball or medicine ball to another child, or one holds the ball while the other tries to push it

- have potato sack races and wheelbarrow races (one child holds the legs of another and the 'barrow' walks along on hands)

- crawl or walk like a crab, hop like a frog, creep like a lizard, wiggle like a snake

- have a giant exercise ball rolled on top of him while lying on the floor

- play tug of war, parachute games, leapfrog, row on a machine

- move desks when necessary, stack chairs, place chairs on desks for cleaning, move gym mats, clean desks and boards; use of both hands should be encouraged

- tie a stretchy band between the front legs of his chair so he can push his legs and feet against it

- jump on mini-trampoline, trampoline, exercise ball, pogo stick, hopping ball, skipping rope, old mattress in a back corner

- return a pile of books to the library or collect reams of paper from the office

- crawl through a fabric tunnel or push a heavy ball through the tunnel

- swim, and maybe wear wrist weights in swimming lessons

- wear wrist and ankle weights in gym class

- water the class plants with a watering can

- raise/lower the flag at school

- push a 'heavy cart'. This could be a two-wheeled trolley or four-wheeled version. Load it up with weighted objects so it takes effort to push or pull. Then create a reason why the child has to push it around. Perhaps it could be where the class returns their library books, or sports equipment. Even if there is only one extra thing on the cart, the child has to push the cart to the library or sports room. Alternatively it could hold things specific to the child, such as a swivel seat or fidget toys, but is kept in a different part of the school – the library, perhaps. Each day the child must collect the trolley and return it later in the day.

Activities to suck, chew and blow

These give sensory input to promote body awareness in the neck, jaw and head:

- Provide age-appropriate items to chew, such as chew toys, chew necklaces or chewing gum. Chewing gum is a wonderful help to children with proprioceptive problems. Teach them to dispose of it properly, of course, but if the school rule is no chewing gum, then try to get an exemption for your student. It really does help.

- Allow the child to have a water bottle on his desk with a straw, the more wriggly the straw the better.

- Play straw-blowing games, such as cotton-ball soccer.

- Play a game where the child has to suck peas to the end of a straw and drop them into a separate bowl. The one with the most peas in the bowl wins.

- Make art pieces by blowing watery paint onto paper.

- Blow bubbles.

- Blow up balloons. Be aware that children with audio sensitivities may be afraid of balloons in case they burst.

Fine motor activities

These build up muscle and joint strength and give sensory input to promote body awareness:

- lacing boards
- beading
- paper tearing
- using tweezers
- play-dough, putty, clay or anything that requires moulding and kneading with hands
- stress and fidget toys and vibrating toys that can be used at any time
- scissor cutting; with an indelible marker, mark a line on the scissors' cutting edge stopping about a centimetre from the end so a child knows when to stop the pressure of cutting and does not close the scissors with every snip
- drawing, painting, colouring
- jigsaw puzzles
- using locks and keys.

Classroom activities

- Have the children lie flat on their backs with their arms straight by their sides, as stiff as a board. Don't let them relax. See how long they can hold that position until they start to feel uncomfortable and begin to squirm. Explain to them that for some people, sitting in a chair, or in one position for even more than a minute or two, feels so uncomfortable that they have to move to relieve the stress.

- Have the children put on pot-holders, or thick oven gloves, and then pour a glass of water from a bottle into a foam or soft plastic cup and then drink the water. Discuss how difficult it is to judge how hard or softly to hold things and how easy it would be to squeeze the cup too hard or drop it because it was not held hard enough.

Home link

Discuss the body awareness issues with parents and caregivers. Communicate the things that you find helpful in the classroom and encourage them to share with you things that have helped at home. Suggest the following things that a parent can do at home:

- Use activities that encourage children to push or pull heavy things such as a lawn mower, take the rubbish to the bins, pull the rubbish bins to the kerb, vacuum, sweep, mop, push a wheelbarrow or shopping trolley, shovel sand or dirt or snow, dig, hoe, rake, pull weeds, water plants with a watering can, clean windows, carry groceries, carry a laundry basket.

- Encourage their child to drink through straws; the curlier the better as the harder the child has to suck then the greater the sensory feedback. Let them also suck thick liquids, such as puddings, jellies, custard, melted ice-cream and apple sauce.

- After-school activities that can assist children with proprioceptive issues include wrestling, horse riding, martial arts, lifting weights and jogging.

- Lying in a hammock can give children the comforting pressure of an all-over body hug.

- Instead of driving a child to school, can he walk or ride a bike? Or if driving, park a long way from the classroom and let him walk to class. If the child takes a bus, if possible and safe, allow him to get off one stop early and walk the rest of the way.

- Encourage the child to ride a bike, or push a scooter or skate or roller blade.

- Let him climb trees.

- Let him help with cooking, especially stirring, beating, whisking and kneading.

- Provide chewy foods for lunch, such as dried fruit, beef jerky, popcorn, muesli/granola bars, carrots, apples.

- Encourage learning wind instruments where he has to blow to make a sound.

Pain

Description

Pain is the body's reaction to stimuli which may cause the body harm. Put simply, nerve endings tell the nervous system which tells the brain that something hurts, so the brain tells the nervous system to tell the nerves of the body part in danger to move away from the danger or alerts the body that something is wrong. Pain is vital to a healthy body. It is also a strange sensation in that only the person who is experiencing the pain can describe what it feels like, and pain levels can differ considerably between people and situations. When the pain system is not working properly then the person can either get heightened messages of pain from very little stimuli, or alternatively be able to endure great pain without the body being aware of it.

People on the autism spectrum often have mixed-up pain systems. They can be *hypersensitive* or *hyposensitive* to pain. However, many children can have strange combinations of both, and their reactions may vary from day to day and situation to situation. Often they can experience both over-reaction to slight pain stimuli and under-reaction to major pain stimuli.

Hypersensitive means that the pain system is over-responsive and the child may experience a disproportionate amount of pain from stimuli. The child:

- may cry or be distressed over a seemingly small injury or hurt, such as a paper cut or splinter

- may feel the cold or heat more than others

- may react in pain from a light touch on the skin.

Hyposensitive means that the pain system is under-responsive and the child does not appear to be bothered by pain in the same way as others. The child:

- may show very little distress at what others would consider major injuries or illnesses

- may ignore major injuries, such as a broken bone, and be able to continue normal activities

- may not be bothered by cold or heat.

HOW YOUR STUDENT MAY EXPLAIN IT

🔆 People tell me I am weird. I can cry with a paper cut and then injure myself really badly and not notice. I had a broken arm twice and mum didn't take me to the doctor for a week both times because I told her it didn't hurt.

🔆 I am always being told to put on a jacket when it is cold, but I don't see the point. I don't feel cold and besides the jacket is heavy and scratchy.

🔆 I love playing rough games where I can bump into other people. I love the feeling it gives me. But when they bump into me, especially if I am not expecting it, it hurts so much I cry. I don't know why this happens. It's so frustrating and I feel stupid, and people say I am a spoil-sport, but I can't help it. I really, really hurt.

At school

The most important thing you can do as a teacher is simply be aware that your student with Asperger's may have unusual responses to pain:

- The child who is hypersensitive to pain may over-react to what others see as a very minor injury. The child is then often branded a cry-baby or a wimp and this can cause bullying in the school ground. Protect this child and realize that the pain felt may be considerable and the child is not a wimp but rather just a child in great pain. If appropriate, and with parental permission, educate the rest of the class on how the pain receptors for this child are different. However, be cautious with this knowledge as it may make the child a target for bullies once they know they can hurt 'the wimp' with minimum effort.

- If your child cries after a minor bump, injury, sting or cut, treat the pain seriously. Protect the child so she is not hurt more. Apply first aid of soothing creams, or ice or heat packs. Distract the child from the injury.

- Sometimes the child will be very rough with others, bumping into them and playing aggressively, and then as soon as she is bumped or pushed back, she cries. The reason may be that the hard bumps she gives may be very enjoyable as they assist in helping the child feel her own body space (proprioception). Or they may give input for the child who has balance (vestibular system) issues. The child with touch hypersensitivities may simply not feel pain from hard knocks and bumps and not realize they might hurt others.

  Also when a child with sensory issues is in control, then she can tolerate high levels of input. But when the bumps and knocks are happening to her and are out of her control, then the pain receptors seem to switch and suddenly the child may feel a lot of pain or get dizzy or frightened from the movement. Other children may regard this child as a hypocrite and ostracize her for these behaviours. If this happens, take the child aside. Explain to her that if choosing to play roughly with other children she is most likely to get hurt most. Discuss other ways to play that do not involve physical contact. Help the child understand that her own behaviours will affect how others deal with her.

- Be aware that some children with Asperger's can endure considerable amounts of pain without showing distress. It has been known for these children to walk on broken legs or use broken arms for days after an injury. Some children do not complain of ear pain until the eardrum has almost burst, or simply be a bit restless as her appendix swells inside them. For this reason is it essential that you get to know your student. Talk to parents about pain history. If you suspect that the child is unwell, even if she does not complain, then be sure to inform caregivers at the end of the day. If the child has had a fall or accident, watch her closely for signs of serious injury. If the child does complain of pain, take it very, very seriously and react immediately. It may even save that child's life.

- Extremes of reactions to input can be due to a build-up of tension or overload. The tired, emotional, fearful, excited child is much more likely to either experience pain from minor injuries or feel pain less. Try to modulate your classroom so that the child's senses are not overloaded. Allow the child regular breaks either to run off extra energy or to be still in a quiet place.

- Be aware that your student may genuinely not feel the cold or heat too much or be bothered by it. Your student may wear a jacket on a hot day and no jacket on a cold day. This may not be much of a problem at school unless the child is in danger from extremes. If the child is dehydrated from overheating in a warm jacket in a heat wave, then steps must be taken to encourage the her to remove the jacket or to drink water and stay in the shade. Likewise if the child is in danger of frostbite or hypothermia from not wearing warm clothes in freezing temperatures, then again steps must be taken to ensure her safety. However, generally, let the child wear whatever makes her comfortable.

- A child may be unaware that she is sick and may be very pale and listless or have a very high temperature. Take note of hot flushed complexions or extreme paleness, and treat the child as sick even if she insists she is fine.

Classroom activity

As there is a chance that any activity to assist children to understand pain may be misinterpreted by parents and school authorities, and might be unappreciated by the students themselves, it was decided that no activities involving pain would be included here.

Home link

- If you suspect that your student is displaying unusual responses to pain then inform the child's caregiver. In many cases knowledge and awareness is all that is needed and both you and the caregiver can assist the child when needed. However, in extreme cases that child may need professional help from an occupational therapist or other health provider.

- Encourage the caregiver to take pain seriously. If a child complains about a minor injury then most likely the child is in real pain. If the child who rarely complains suddenly mentions feeling sick or hurt, take it very seriously and seek medical care as soon as possible.

Synaesthesia

Description

Synaesthesia is an unusual and curious condition. Basically it is where a person experiences a sensation with one sense but then converts it into another sense. The word in its Greek roots means coming together of senses. For example, a child may 'see' music as a kaleidoscope of colour, or hear a word that gives them a physical sensation of velvet or gravel. Often synaesthetes can see numbers in colour and so 1 may be white and 5 may be red. However, it is not as simple as seeing a white 1 or a red 5. It is as if the number *is* the colour. Many people with and without Asperger Syndrome experience synaesthesia, often without even realizing it. Just as a person with colour blindness may not realize for years that everyone else sees colours differently from her, synaesthetes often believe that everyone sees and experiences the world in the same way that they do.

One of the most famous synaesthetes is Daniel Tammet, author of *Born on a Blue Day*. Daniel can recall the number pi to 22,514 decimal places and can do extraordinarily difficult mathematical problems in his mind. However, he doesn't calculate the answers. He *sees* the answers in patterns and colours.

An even rarer condition is known as mirror-touch synaesthesia, where, if another person gets touched, the synaesthete feels a touch on her body in a mirrored image. So if someone gets hurt on her right arm, the person with mirror-touch synaesthesia feels the pain in her own left arm.

HOW YOUR STUDENT MAY EXPLAIN IT

Synaesthesia

- When I tell people that I feel sounds, they think it is rather neat, but I don't think of it that way, it's just how I am. I don't think they are 'neat' because they can see a tree. When I hear words that give nice feelings like silky or velvety or milky, then that is good and pleasant. But some words feel horrible, like gravel or like a spider running over my body. Some music can 'sound' fine, but give me the feeling of slime being poured over me, which makes me physically sick. The worst thing is that I can't control the words others will say or the sounds around me, so I never know how I will feel from one minute to the next. If I am already overloaded with other things then the sound feelings are even stronger.

- I can see numbers as colours. When I do a maths sum, I know the answer is right if the colour of the answer is right. The colours of right answers are beautiful and harmonious.

Mirror-touch synaesthesia

- I hate watching movies or situations where people are violent towards one another. I feel all the pain of the person getting hurt. Also watching people kiss is quite disturbing for me. There are definitely sensations I do not want to share with others.

At school

As a teacher you do not have to do anything particular about synaesthesia in your classroom other than be aware that it exists and there is a slight chance that your student with Asperger Syndrome may experience it. If you suspect that your student has this condition then talk to her about what she is experiencing. The child herself may well think that everyone else sees and experiences the world in the same way she does, and not even realize she has this unusual condition. Use prudence about sharing the knowledge of the child's synaesthesia with others. Little harm can come if it is known that the child sees 1 as white, but if other children or unkind adults know that a certain word or type of music or visual image can cause physical distress, then it is open to abuse.

If necessary, adapt your classroom to accommodate any problems that may arise for the child. For example, if you know that a certain word you use regularly causes the child to feel spiders run over her body, then don't use that word. As in all cases of people with sensory disorders, overload exacerbates the situation; so try to make your classroom a calm, ordered safe place for all children. In extreme cases, medical specialists may need to be consulted.

Classroom activity

Important: Only discuss your student's synaesthesia in the classroom with full support of the child and the caregiver and if you are sure it will not expose the child to bullying.

- Have the class close their eyes and listen to some evocative music. Often sound tracks for movies are written deliberately to elicit an emotional response. Discuss what they 'see' when they hear the music. Talk about images that come to mind and things they feel. Talk about how the things they feel and 'see' when listening to this music come from their own experiences. Perhaps they saw the movie the music came from and saw starships battling each other. Maybe they were feeling very sad that day and the music made them sadder. Then talk about how some people can 'see' images or shapes or colours when they hear sounds, but what they see is not learned and does not change with emotions. It is as if a particular sound *is* yellow, for example. Discuss how that would change the way they saw the world. Discuss positives and negatives of this condition.

Home link

If you suspect your student has synaesthesia, then discuss this with the child's caregiver. Work together to create an environment at home and at school where the child is safe and protected from any overload or abuse that may arise from this condition. Work together to build up the child's self-esteem through this unusual gift.

REFERENCES

American Psychiatric Association (2013) *Diagnostic and Statistical Manual of Mental Disorders, 5th Edition.* Washington DC: American Psychiatric Association.

Tammet, D. (2007) *Born on a Blue Day.* London: Hodder Paperbacks.

Books that explain Asperger Syndrome to children

Durà-Vilà, G. and Levi, T. (2014) *My Autism Book: A Child's Guide to their Autism Spectrum Diagnosis.* London: Jessica Kingsley Publishers.

Hoopmann, K. (2000) *Blue Bottle Mystery.* London: Jessica Kingsley Publishers.

Hoopmann, K. (2001) *Of Mice and Aliens.* London: Jessica Kingsley Publishers.

Hoopmann, K. (2002) *Lisa and the Lacemaker.* London: Jessica Kingsley Publishers.

Hoopmann, K. (2003) *Haze.* London: Jessica Kingsley Publishers.

Hoopmann, K. (2006) *All Cats have Asperger Syndrome.* London: Jessica Kingsley Publishers.

Welton, J. (2003) *Can I tell you about Asperger's Syndrome?* London: Jessica Kingsley Publishers.

Welton, J. (2014) *Can I tell you about Autism?* London: Jessica Kingsley Publishers.

Books that explain Asperger Syndrome to teachers and parents

Attwood, T. (2008) *The Complete Guide to Asperger's Syndrome.* London: Jessica Kingsley Publishers.

Boyd, B. (2009) *Appreciating Asperger Syndrome.* London: Jessica Kingsley Publishers.

Bradshaw, S. and Happé, F. (2012) *Asperger's Syndrome – That Explains Everything: Strategies for Education, Life and Just About Everything Else.* London: Jessica Kingsley Publishers.

MacKenzie, H. (2008) *Reaching and Teaching the Child with Autism Spectrum Disorder.* London: Jessica Kingsley Publishers.

Notbohm, E. and Zysk, V. (2010) *1001 Great Ideas for Teaching and Raising Children with Autism and Asperger's.* Arlington, TX: Future Horizons.

Robison, J.E. (2011) *Be Different.* New York: Random House.

Santomauro, J. and Carter, M. (2009) *Your Special Student: A Book for Educators of Children Diagnosed with Asperger Syndrome.* London: Jessica Kingsley Publishers.

Winter, M. (2011) *Asperger Syndrome: What Teachers Need to Know.* London: Jessica Kingsley Publishers.